In the Lions' Den

and

The Panther

Studies in Austrian Literature, Culture and Thought
Translation Series

General Editors:

Jorun B. Johns
Richard H. Lawson

Felix Mitterer

In the Lions' Den
Translated by Victoria Martin

and

The Panther
Translated by Mike Lyons, Patrick Drysdale, Dennis McCort

Preface by Felix Mitterer
Afterword by Gerd K. Schneider
Edited by Dennis McCort

Ariadne Press
Riverside, California

Ariadne Press would like to express its appreciation to the Bundesministerium für Unterricht, Kunst und Kultur for assistance in publishing this book.

.KUNST

Translated from the German
In der Löwengrube, Der Panther
Book rights ©Haymon Verlag, Innsbruck-Wien
Performance Rights ©Österreichischer Bühnenverlag Kaiser & Co.

Library of Congress Cataloging-in-Publication Data

Mitterer, Felix, 1948-
 [In der Löwengrube. English]
 In the lions' den, and The panther / Felix Mitterer ; translated by Victoria Martin, Mike Lyons, Patrick Drysdale, Dennis McCort ; preface by Felix Mitterer ; afterword by Gerd K. Schneider ; edited by Dennis McCort.
   p. cm. -- (Studies in Austrian literature, culture and thought. Translation series)
 ISBN 978-1-57241-180-7
 1. Mitterer, Felix, 1948---Translations into English. 2. Jews—Persecutions --- Austria--Tyrol--Drama. 3. Holocaust, Jewish (1939-1945)--Austria--Drama. 4. Tyrol (Austria)--History--Drama. I. Martin, Victoria. II. Lyons, Mike. III. Drysdale, Patrick. IV. McCort, Dennis. V. Title.
 PT2673.I79I613 2011
 832'.914--dc22   2011014148

Cover Design
George McGinnis

Copyright 2011
by Ariadne Press
270 Goins Court
Riverside, CA 92507

All rights reserved.
No part of this publication may be reproduced or transmitted
in any form or by any means without formal permission.
Printed in the United States of America.
ISBN 978-1-57241-180-7

Contents

Preface by Felix Mitterer

In the Lions' Den 1

   Translated by Victoria Martin

The Panther 129

   Translated by Mike Lyons, Patrick Drysdale and Dennis McCort

Afterword 195

   Gerd K. Schneider

Acknowledgments

My gratitude to Professors Gerlinde Sanford († 2010) and Gerd K. Schneider for bringing the works of Felix Mitterer to my attention. –D. McC.

Grateful thanks are due to Frau Ingrid Rogy (Maedi) who ten years or so ago gave me a copy of Felix Mitterer's *Sibirien*. This marked the start of my admiration for the work of Felix Mitterer and of a sequence of events leading to the publication of this book. –M. L.

Preface

In 1999 and 2003, I was treated to two unusual theater performances given in English, both at the Unicorn Theater in Abingdon, Oxfordshire. The first performance was of *In the Lions' Den,* translated and directed by Victoria Martin. The piece has an authentic background and deals with the destiny of the Jewish actor Leo Reuss, who, upon being banned from the stage by the Nazis, went missing for a year, only to reappear as a Tyrolean peasant farmer and celebrate a great triumph on stage as an Aryan "natural." In 1938 Leo Reuss emigrated to America where he was limited to playing Nazi henchmen in Hollywood movies, which gave him little pleasure. To be sure, some had it in mind to make a film of his great feat of leading the Nazis around by the nose, but a peculiar linguistic problem arose preventing it. How was the English language to deal with the matter of Reuss's return as a country bumpkin speaking Tyrolean dialect? No solution could be found and so the film was never made. Too bad the Hollywood producers couldn't come up with an idea like that of Victoria Martin. In her production a man with a full beard and wearing Tyrolean garb takes the stage – and what does he speak? He speaks an amazing Scottish brogue. Therewith all became clear; the public immediately understood what was going on.

The second performance was of *Siberia,* translated by Michael Lyons and Patrick Drysdale. In it Tom Bewley gave a most impressive performance as the old man in the nursing home who struggles to attain a dignified departure from this world.

The famous actor Fritz Muliar had played this role over two hundred times at the Vienna Akademietheater, becoming a legend in the process. Some years ago when Fritz Muliar celebrated the seventieth anniversary of his life on stage, I wrote the play *The Panther* for him and in his honor. This play too has now been translated into English, by Michael Lyons, Patrick Drysdale and Dennis McCort. And with this the circle closes.

My heartfelt thanks go to Victoria, Mike, Paddy and Dennis, as well as to Gerd K. Schneider and our esteemed publisher Jorun Johns.

Felix Mitterer

In the Lions' Den

Translated by

Victoria Martin

© Victoria Martin April 2010

In the Lions' Den

CAST OF CHARACTERS:

ARTHUR KIRSCH, alias BENEDIKT HÖLLRIGL
HELENE SCHWAIGER, his wife, the star of the ensemble
MEISEL, the theater manager and director
POLACEK, an actor
STRASSKY, an actor
MOROVITZ, an actor
OLGA STERNBERG, an actress
EDER, the stage manager
FIRST GESTAPO OFFICER
GOEBBELS, the Nazi Minister for Propaganda
BENEDIKT HÖLLRIGL, the real one

Various ACTORS, STAGE CREW, PROMPTER, ANOTHER GESTAPO OFFICER, SA and SS MEN, A FILM CREW and REPORTERS (all extras)

LOCATION: Vienna, the stage of a theater

TIME: Shortly before, during and one year after the Nazi seizure of power

SCENE 1

The curtain rises on the set for the "Merchant of Venice," Act 3, Scene 1, Venice. Polacek (as Solanio) and Strassky (as Salarino) enter.

POLACEK as SOLANIO: Now, what news on the Rialto?

STRASSKY as SALARINO: Why, yet it lives there unchecked that Antonio hath a ship of rich lading wrecked on the narrow seas – the Goodwins I think they call the place – a very dangerous flat and fatal, where the carcasses of many a tall ship lie buried, as they say, if my gossip report be an honest woman of her word.

POLACEK as SOLANIO: I would she were as lying a gossip in that as ever knapped ginger or made her neighbors believe she wept for the death of a third husband. But it is true, without any slips of prolixity or crossing the plain highway of talk, that the good Antonio, the honest Antonio, – O that I had a title good enough to keep his name company! –

STRASSKY as SALARINO: Come, the full stop.

POLACEK as SOLANIO: Ha! What say'st thou? Why, the end is, he hath lost a ship.

STRASSKY as SALARINO: I would it might prove the end of his losses.

POLACEK as SOLANIO: Let me say "Amen" betimes, lest the devil cross my prayer, for here he comes in the likeness of a Jew.

Kirsch enters as Shylock. Someone in the audience whistles.

POLACEK as SOLANIO: How now, Shylock! What news among the merchants?

KIRSCH as SHYLOCK: You knew, none so well, none so well as you, of my daughter's flight.

STRASSKY as SALARINO: That's certain. I for my part knew the tailor that made the wings she flew withal.

POLACEK as SOLANIO: And Shylock for his own part knew the bird was fledg'd; and then it is the complexion of them all to leave the dam.

KIRSCH as SHYLOCK: She is damned for it.

Another whistle.

STRASSKY as SALARINO: That's certain, if the devil may be her judge.

KIRSCH as SHYLOCK: My own flesh and blood to rebel!

POLACEK as SOLANIO: Out upon it, old carrion, rebels it at these years?

KIRSCH as SHYLOCK: I say my daughter is my flesh and blood.

STRASSKY as SALARINO: There is more difference between thy flesh and hers than between jet and ivory; more between your bloods than there is between red wine and Rhenish.

A number of men laugh scornfully. Someone shouts "Bravo!"

STRASSKY as SALARINO: (*continues*) But tell us, do you hear whether Antonio have had any loss at sea or no?

KIRSCH as SHYLOCK: There I have another bad match. A bankrupt, a prodigal, who dare scarce show his head on the Rialto; a beggar, that was used to come so smug upon the mart. Let him look to his bond. He was wont to call me a usurer: let him look to his bond. He was wont to lend money for a Christian courtesy: let him look to his bond.

Two members of the audience whistle.

STRASSKY as SALARINO: A pound of flesh, nearest the heart.

KIRSCH as SHYLOCK: So is the penalty, which thus appeareth due upon the bond.

STRASSKY as SALARINO: Why, I am sure, if he forfeit, thou wilt not take his flesh. What's that good for?

KIRSCH as SHYLOCK: To bait fish withal. If it will feed nothing else, it will feed my revenge.

Four members of the audience whistle.

KIRSCH as SHYLOCK: (*continues*) He hath disgraced me, and hindered me half a million; laughed at my losses, mocked at my gains, scorned my nation, thwarted my bargains, cooled my friends, heated mine enemies. And what's his reason? I am a Jew.

A chorus of whistles and yells of protest from some of the audience. The noise lasts so long that it is scarcely possible to hear Kirsch. Until now the actors have not reacted to the audience's behavior, now Polacek and

Strassky look at them. Kirsch raises his voice and speaks his lines with genuine anger, but at first still addressing his fellow actors.

KIRSCH as SHYLOCK: (*continues*) Hath not a Jew eyes? Hath not a Jew hands, organs, dimensions, senses, affections, passions; fed with the same food, hurt with the same weapons, subject to the same diseases, healed by the same means, warmed and cooled by the same winter and summer, as a Christian is? If you prick us, do we not bleed? If you tickle us, do we not laugh? If you poison us, do we not die? And if you wrong us, shall we not revenge? If we are like you in the rest, we will resemble you in that. If a Jew wrong a Christian, what is his humility? Revenge. If a Christian wrong a Jew, what would his sufferance be by Christian example? Why, revenge.

The curtain falls. The whistling and cries of protest stop and instead we hear cheers and applause from the protesters. They fall silent. Lights go up slightly in the auditorium. Meisel steps in front of the curtain. He is a nervous, distracted man, who lives on tranquillizers.

MEISEL: Now, now, please, no really, this really won't do.

Continuous whistling and booing, which grows louder.

MEISEL: Gentlemen, this is, I mean, consider where you are, you can't simply let your feelings, please, stop this, we value our regular audience, they have the right to, remember this is a premiere, you, I shall call the police, this is unacceptable behavior, this is not an opera house after all. You're acting like louts, yes, louts all of you, what kind of behavior is this, this is a civilized place, a temple of culture, kindly understand. Quiet, quiet please, this has never happened before, never, unbelievable, ladies and gentlemen, esteemed members of the audience, I very much regret that we are compelled to postpone, this performance has been postponed.

Meisel disappears behind the curtain, the protesters cheer and clap. Lights go up fully in the auditorium. After a while the curtain rises, working lights on stage, in the auditorium the lights go down. The cast together with Meisel are on stage: Kirsch (as Shylock), Polacek (as Solanio), Strassky (as Salarino), Morovitz (as Bassanio), Olga (as Jessica) and extras as Lancelot Gobbo, Antonio and Lorenzo, also the stage manager Eder and his crew. Polacek and Strassky are enjoying the situation.

MEISEL: (*running about*) A disaster, a disaster, disastrous, absolutely disastrous, this means ruin!

The actors (extras) playing the Duke of Venice, the Prince of Morocco, the Prince of Aragon, Gratiano, Tubal, Old Gobbo, Leonardo, Balthasar, Stephano and Nerissa come on stage.

MEISEL: (*to Kirsch*) I ought to throw you out, Kirsch! How could he? Ruins my theater!

Kirsch stands hanging his head like a beaten dog. His wife, Helene Schwaiger, comes on stage as Portia, every inch the star.

MEISEL: Ruins my theater, this man ruins my theater, this nobody ruins my theater, my life's work!

HELENE: He wasn't all that bad! Really, I don't understand.

MEISEL: You're fired, Kirsch.

HELENE: (*threateningly*) I wouldn't do that if I were you, Herr Meisel.

The prompter tries to climb out of her box. The actor playing Tubal (an extra) helps her.

MEISEL: There's never been such a, it's unbelievable, we can't afford, do you know the state of our finances? I try to keep feeding this huge mob, I try to perform Shakespeare with hundreds of actors, fool that I am, and who do I have in the main role? An amateur, yes, Herr Kirsch, an amateur. You're fired, Kirsch, as of now.

Kirsch nods humbly.

MEISEL: (*to Helene*) This adventure, Frau Schwaiger, you talked me into, you pleaded with me on bended knee until ..., you even threatened to resign, you, no, let's call it by its proper name, you black–

HELENE: It's his twenty-fifth anniversary! Twenty-five years treading the boards! On an occasion like this one can afford to –

MEISEL: Twenty-five years of minor roles and then Shylock! A supporting actor has never played, it's madness, Frau Schwaiger, and I had to let him, out of the goodness of my, and look what's come of it, look what, it serves me right.

OLGA: I've had enough of this. He's good, he's good, Herr Kirsch is superb as Shylock, fantastic. How can you be so cruel? You've all got eyes in your heads, you've got ears. Why are you just standing there and not speaking up for him?

MEISEL: Fräulein Sternberg, would you please? What we have just heard, that was the voice of the people, and that's all that, only money at the box office counts, that's all! Or do you all want to find yourselves on the street, is that what you want?

OLGA: That isn't the voice of the people, Herr Meisel, you know that perfectly well, you all do! They're scum, politically motivated scum!

MEISEL: (*to Olga*) I have no idea what you're –

STRASSKY: (*interrupts by yelling at Olga*) You will not call the German people politically motivated scum, do you understand?

Olga starts, stares at Strassky in amazement.

MEISEL: Herr Strassky, might I ask you not to shout on my, if anyone is going to shout on my stage, then it's me, but I am not shouting, because this is not a menagerie, it is –

STRASSKY: (*grins*) A temple of culture, I know.

MEISEL: It is, and it will stay that, however, would someone please explain to me what's, I mean, what you're talking about, Fräulein Sternberg, you can't be –

POLACEK: Herr Meisel, we've warned you before, haven't we? It isn't a question of Herr Kirsch's thespian qualities, Fräulein Sternberg is right about that. It's a question of his – racial affinities. You know only too well that they aren't exactly in demand at the moment, don't you?

MEISEL: Well, really, Herr Polacek. Might I draw your attention to the fact that it's "The Merchant of Venice" we're performing?!

STRASSKY: Right – and next it'll be Othello with a genuine black. Realism is everything, right, Herr Meisel?

MEISEL: I'm a good man, you all know that! Too compliant, much too, what am I going to do now, what am I going to do now? This is an expensive, a vastly expensive production, I can't just cancel it.

STRASSKY: Listen to me, Herr Meisel, we'll save the day. We care about this theater just as much as you do.

MEISEL: Save? Yes, how, how, Strassky?

STRASSKY: The part will be recast and the production tailored to the spirit of the modern age. Herr Polacek can handle all that.

MEISEL: You'd do that?

POLACEK: (*grins*) Of course, Herr Meisel. I'll give you the Shylock to end all Shylocks.

MEISEL: Well then, let's, I hardly dare, at any rate, thank you, gentlemen, I'm extremely grateful. In the meantime we'll re-run "The Rape of the Sabine Women." Good night, that's it for this evening. (*To the stage manager:*) Get this set out of my sight, Eder, what I have to go through in this theater, honestly!

EDER: Right away, Herr Meisel.

Meisel exits, then all the others, until only Kirsch, Helene and Morovitz are left. Kirsch sits down, depressed. The stage crew begin to dismantle the set.

MOROVITZ: You were terrific, Arthur, I just wanted you to know that.

KIRSCH: Thanks, Gernot.

MOROVITZ: (*pounds him on the shoulder*) Well then, good luck. You'll come through. You're a survivor.

Morovitz starts to leave, then stops upstage, looks questioningly at Helene and points backstage (asking if they can meet there). Helene makes an impatient negative gesture, Morovitz goes off.

KIRSCH: (*laughs*) What a fool I am! I should have stuck to my minor roles. But no, I wanted to be in the limelight. Vaulting ambition which o'erleaps itself! It serves me right.

HELENE: Arthur, I'm afraid I've got to – I've got another meeting about the film. They want to foist that dreadful cameraman on me again, the one who always shoots me from my worst side. Will you go home to the children?

KIRSCH: Yes, I'll go home to the children.

HELENE: All right – I might be late, don't worry about me. (*Goes upstage, turns round.*) You can forget about being fired. Meisel needs me.

She goes off. Kirsch sits there alone. Eder looks at him and comes over.

EDER: Herr Kirsch.

Kirsch looks up.

EDER: (*he has a strong working class accent*) I just wanted to say that you're a bloody good actor. You can't fool me, I've been in this business long enough. I hear every false note backstage there. Every one. And I hear a lot of 'em, every night. But not with you. Not even if you've only got two lines in the whole bloody play.

KIRSCH: (*very pleased*) Thank you, Herr Eder.

EDER: If I was in your shoes I'd take this whole disruption as a compliment.

KIRSCH: That's easy to say.

EDER: We've got to tidy up here, Herr Kirsch. Sorry.

KIRSCH: I'm on my way. Thanks, Herr Eder, good night. (*Exits.*)

EDER: Night, Herr Kirsch. (*Goes off to the side and closes the curtain.*)

SCENE 2

Meisel is sitting in the auditorium, the curtain rises, no set. The cast are rehearsing their new parts. Polacek is now acting in the make-up and costume of Shylock, Kirsch plays Tubal. Polacek plays Shylock as an anti-Semitic caricature, speaking with an exaggerated Fagin-like Yiddish accent; his make-up is in accordance with this interpretation. Kirsch also has an exaggeratedly anti-Semitic costume and make-up but acts the part "normally"; he does not adopt a Yiddish accent.

POLACEK as SHYLOCK: How now, Tubal! What news from Genoa? Hast thou found my daughter?

KIRSCH as TUBAL: I often came where I did hear of her, but cannot find her.

POLACEK: (*in a not unfriendly manner*) Arthur, Arthur, you

can't play it like that, seriously. (*Looks to Meisel.*)

MEISEL: (*gets up, walks over to the apron*) Kirsch, come here.

Kirsch comes downstage.

MEISEL: Did I sack you, Kirsch? No, I did not sack you, my generosity prevailed and I, so, will you cooperate? No, you will not cooperate.

KIRSCH: Herr Meisel –

MEISEL: You have ONE scene, ONE scene, you must be able to, I mean –

KIRSCH: I can't Jew it up, I can't! That's not what Shakespeare intended!

POLACEK: And you know how they played it back then, do you?

KIRSCH: I don't care how they played it back then. We're doing it now.

POLACEK: Exactly! It's an anti-Semitic play, Arthur! It was played that way then and it must be played that way again now. YOU wanted to make a piece of Jewish propaganda out of it, it was bound to go wrong!

MEISEL: Kirsch, you chose this play yourself, so will you please get on with it; either you knuckle down, or I'll throw you and your wife, she shouldn't get it into her head that she's the only star in this, she couldn't be more wrong!

POLACEK: Arthur! You know how things stand. If you get

kicked out of here, you'll never find another engagement, no other theater will take you.

MEISEL: Come on, get on with it, I don't have time to spare, I'm not only the director you know, I have to support this whole, like Atlas, you have no idea! (*Takes a pill, sits down.*)

POLACEK as SHYLOCK: Why, there, there, there, there. A diamond gone cost me two thousand ducats in Frankfurt. The curse never fell upon our nation till now; I never felt it till now. Two thousand ducats in that and other precious, precious jewels! I would my daughter were dead at my foot and the jewels in her ear! Would she were hearsed at my foot and the jewels in her coffin!

SA men with truncheons come on stage. They stay in the background, watching. They include Strassky and Morovitz. Kirsch sees them and is frightened. Polacek sees them and starts to ham it up. Meisel also sees them but ignores them.

POLACEK as SHYLOCK: (*continues*) No news of them? Why, so. And I know not what's spent in the search. Why, thou – loss upon loss! The thief gone with so much, and so much to find the thief, and no satisfaction, no revenge, nor no ill luck stirring but what lights o' my shoulders, no sighs but o' my breathing, no tears but o' my shedding.

The SA men applaud.

KIRSCH as TUBAL. (*now also with a Yiddish accent*) Yes, other men have ill luck too. Antonio, as I heard in Genoa –

POLACEK as SHYLOCK: What, what, what? Ill luck, ill luck?

KIRSCH as TUBAL: Hath an argosy cast away, coming from Tripolis.

MEISEL: (*stands up*) Thank you, that will suffice, just keep it up, you see, Kirsch, you can do it, now will you please excuse, thank you, gentlemen (*Tries to leave.*)

STRASSKY: (*coming downstage*) Herr Meisel!

MEISEL: (*turns round*) Ah, Herr Strassky, in uniform today I see, smart, very smart, some kind of parade today, festivities? Congratulations, now if I might –

STRASSKY: Herr Meisel!

MEISEL: Yes?

STRASSKY: Your absent-mindedness is an endearing trait, Herr Meisel, but would you please try to concentrate for once.

MEISEL: Well, what is it then, Strassky? What a serious expression, I take it you've been promoted, eh, my heartiest congratulations, and now if I might –

STRASSKY: (*shouts*) Shut your mouth, you arsehole!

Meisel freezes.

MOROVITZ: (*comes downstage*) Don't take it badly, Herr Meisel. He didn't mean it like that.

STRASSKY: I fucking well did mean it like that! You little bourgeois shit!

MEISEL: Really, I must ask you to moderate, this is a civilized place, this is really not accept –

STRASSKY: Come here, now!

Meisel goes up the steps onto the stage.

STRASSKY: What's the matter with you? You think we're some kind of Punch and Judy show, do you?

MEISEL: But of course not, Herr Strassky, it never entered my –

STRASSKY: Do you think we're dressed like this for laughs? Do you?

MEISEL: But of course not, why on earth would I, but you know how it is, I'm a creature of the theater, my life is the theater, I know nothing about the outside world, I don't want to know about …, filth, it's all filth out there, no culture, all this is my shelter, this theater here is my carapace, and then naturally everything else becomes just, how shall I put it, backdrop, costume, yes, costume, it all becomes just costume. You must forgive me, Herr Strassky, even this splendid brown uniform is just a costume to me, somehow, we should do a production in this sort of uniform, it looks really splendid, anyone know of a suitable play?

Strassky groans with irritation.

MOROVITZ: We know that you're not interested in the world outside the theater, Herr Meisel. Do you mind if I explain it to you?

MEISEL: Yes, do, please, Herr Morovitz. I must say, this

costume suits you particularly well, this uniform I mean; oh God, you're not all going to leave me and join the army, are you?

MOROVITZ: No, no, you're not going to lose us, Herr Meisel. Now, please listen to me. (*Speaks as if to a child.*) We National Socialists, the National Socialist German Workers' Party, have taken power.

MEISEL: (*hesitates briefly*) Well, that's in order, I'm entirely on your side, congratulations, always was in favor of authoritarian leadership, can't run a theater any other, certainly, that's right.

Helene, Olga and the other actors come on stage, as do Eder and the stage crew, accompanied by an SA man who has fetched them. None are in costume. Helene is dressed in an extremely expensive and fashionable outfit.

STRASSKY: (*after all have come to a standstill*) Herr Meisel, we hereby assume provisional control of the management of this theater. Herr Polacek, Herr Morovitz and myself.

MEISEL: My dear colleagues, don't do this to yourselves, you have no idea, there is nothing worse than running a theater, dreadful, I tell you, act, my friends, act, that is your vocation, not administration!

POLACEK: It's not a question of administration, Herr Meisel, it's a question of ideology.

MEISEL: Absolutely, absolutely, I'm entirely in favor of ideology, what is a theater other than an instrument for –

STRASSKY: (*interrupting*) I know what you mean by ideology,

Herr Meisel! Watered down humanism! Soggy liberal do-gooding! But I'm talking about our steely, virile National Socialist ideology, Herr Meisel! The actor as cultural-political soldier! Down with foreign trash! Down with Jewish trash! German art on the German stage!

MEISEL: Well, yes, I've nothing against –

MOROVITZ: (*cutting him off*) There will be a pay rise in the next season, colleagues, that I can promise you! No more redundancies!

Applause from most of those present.

MEISEL: Well, yes, now there I don't –

MOROVITZ: And since critical reviews express nothing more than Jewish and individualist malice, they are banned from now on. Instead, only objective and constructive Nazi reviews will be allowed. Well, isn't that a relief?

Applause.

POLACEK: Pity, really. Now I can't box any more critics' ears.

Laughter.

STRASSKY: There is one more innovation. From now on, colleagues, we will no longer bow our heads like dogs during the curtain call. We will respond to applause with a salute. Like this! (*Demonstrates a Nazi salute.*) Is that clear? A German does not bow!

MEISEL: Yes, well, actually, I've always found it rather a nice custom, I mean –

STRASSKY: Herr Meisel, you are surplus to requirements. I suggest you take a little holiday. Your office has already been sealed off and we are in the process of checking the accounts. And while you are off sunning yourself, we will muck out this pigsty. You may go. Oh, and don't leave town, we may have need of you. Heil Hitler!

MEISEL: Certainly, greet Hitler (*goes off muttering*), good morning, Heil, call that culture, oh my theater, my poor, don't leave town, I never leave town, you don't need to tell me...

Kirsch stands as if paralysed, not daring to move in case the SA notice him.

STRASSKY: (*looks round the stage and the auditorium*) God, this place stinks. Disgusting! A mixture of cultural bolshevism and rotting bourgeois decadence! But there's something here that smells even worse. Fortunately, that stench is the easiest to deal with. Let's make a start. Anyone here who is not of pure Aryan blood, say loud and clear "I'm not."

POLACEK: (*as Shylock, writhing*) I'm not!

STRASSKY: This is not a laughing matter.

KIRSCH: (*quietly*) I'm not.

STRASSKY: Sorry, I didn't quite get that.

KIRSCH: (*louder*) I'm not.

STRASSKY: I still can't hear.

KIRSCH: (*shouts*) I'm not!

STRASSKY: (*looks at Kirsch, then looks round*) No one else? No? Well, we'll soon find out. (*Yells:*) Never again will a Jewish actor play a German character! Never again will we allow such a disgrace! (*To Kirsch:*) So in a way your last part was the right one, Kirsch. And you've got pretty good at talking like a Yid, you can keep that up.

HELENE: Stop it, Strassky!

STRASSKY: Eder, get me a bucket of water and a scrubbing brush!

EDER: (*stares uncomprehendingly at Strassky, then*) I'm the stage manager, Herr Strassky! (*Goes off*).

STRASSKY: (*yells backstage*) A bucket and a scrubbing brush!

One of the SA men goes off. Helene nudges Morovitz angrily.

MOROVITZ: Chuck him out and forget it, Strassky.

POLACEK: (*who also finds the situation embarrassing*) Yes, come on, Strassky. Hey, Kirsch, what's Shylock's last line?

KIRSCH: I pray you, give me leave to go from hence, I am not well.

POLACEK: Then go, Jew.

Kirsch tries to leave. Strassky blocks his way, grabs him by the shoulder and brings him back. The SA man brings a bucket and brush, Strassky points at Kirsch, the SA man puts the bucket down in front of him.

HELENE: (*comes forward*) Herr Strassky, I am a good friend of Dr. Goebbels, I hope you realize.

STRASSKY: You certainly mention the fact often enough. But I would be interested to know, Frau Schwaiger, if Dr. Goebbels is aware of what you're married to?

Helene hesitates in embarrassment, Strassky enjoys this and turns again to Kirsch.

STRASSKY: For twenty-five years you have sullied this stage with your filthy Jewish feet, Kirsch. So now you will scrub this stage till it gleams, every inch of it. Till it gleams. (*Shouts:*) Is that clear?

KIRSCH: Yes.

Strassky looks at him, then puts his hand to his ear.

KIRSCH: (*loudly*) Yes, sir.

OLGA: Why are you doing this, Hubert?

STRASSKY: We're on a mission from Hitler.

OLGA: How can you call that a mission, humiliating people, attacking your fellow actors?

STRASSKY: Missions are not a children's tea party, young lady! Missions are painful surgical operations. Missions excise diseased organs. They are a process of purification. (*Yells:*) Missions are not lovey-dovey!

OLGA: Then I can do without that sort of mission.

Olga exits. Some of the others try to leave as well.

STRASSKY: (*shouts*) Hey, did I say you could leave? This is an official gathering of the National Socialist Company Management Committee! Kindly remember that!

Everyone but Olga comes back. Eder also reappears and watches angrily, he can hardly contain himself. Strassky looks at Kirsch and taps his truncheon against the palm of his hand. Kirsch looks at his fellow actors, looks at the bucket, then kneels down, dips the brush into the water and begins to clean the floor. Everyone watches silently, almost all the actors are distressed.

STRASSKY: By the way, Kirsch, just to let you know: WE organized that protest action at the premiere, Polacek, Morovitz and myself.

POLACEK: (*almost apologetically*) We couldn't let you get away with that, not on the eve of victory! You do understand that, Arthur, don't you?

Kirsch pauses, looks at Strassky, then Polacek, then Morovitz, who is embarrassed by Strassky's revelation. Kirsch resumes his scrubbing.

HELENE: (*indignantly, to Morovitz*) Oh?

MOROVITZ: (*looks away, ashamed, then to Strassky*) Look, are we going to have to watch this all day?

POLACEK: Come on, Strassky, let's go to the canteen. To be honest, I could do with a smoke.

STRASSKY: Kirsch, I'll be back in an hour to check up. Every inch of it.

He goes off upstage, all but Helene and Eder follow him, Eder watches Strassky go.

EDER: The smaller the talent, the bigger the Nazi. What a bastard! (*Looks at Kirsch*) Forgive me, Herr Kirsch, but I've got my family to think of.

Kirsch looks up at him and nods, Eder goes off. Kirsch continues to scrub the floor, Helene looks at him despairingly, then kneels down next to him and embraces him.

HELENE: What are we going to do, Arthur?

KIRSCH: I'll go away.

HELENE: But where?

KIRSCH: (*still scrubbing*) I don't know yet.

HELENE: (*gets up, sees a water mark on her dress*) Oh God! (*Rubs at it.*) I'll come with you, of course I'll come with you.

KIRSCH: No. Someone has to earn the money. For the sake of the children.

HELENE: Yes, you're right.

KIRSCH: We'll get divorced.

HELENE: Never! I'd die first!

KIRSCH: We have to, otherwise your career is finished. For the sake of the children.

HELENE: You're right. Oh, my clever Arthur! (*Kneels down*

again, but this time further away so that she doesn't get wet. She embraces him with some difficulty. She is constantly playing a part, she can't help herself.) I will always be your loving wife, in my heart.

KIRSCH: Of course.

HELENE: (*gets up*) Go to Switzerland. Take the children with you. Find a good boarding school for them. I've got lots of film offers, I'll accept them all.

KIRSCH: You do that. And now leave me alone for a while.

HELENE: Shall I help you? I'd like to help you.

KIRSCH: No, don't worry. When I think about it, this is something I ought to be pleased to do. I love these boards. Why shouldn't I clean them before I go? (*Gets up, embraces her.*) Goodbye, Helene.

Helene can't suppress a sob, and then can't suppress her delight at having produced such a wonderfully natural sob. She hugs Kirsch, Kirsch frees himself, kneels down again and carries on scrubbing.

HELENE: I'll visit you all in Switzerland, of course.

KIRSCH: That's nice.

Helene goes slowly off, looks back and sobs briefly.

KIRSCH: Leni!

Helene turns around.

KIRSCH: Don't sell out completely, so that you're ashamed of yourself afterwards – although, you'll always be sure you were innocent, I know.

Helene looks at him, feels guilty and deals with it by exploding into anger.

HELENE: Why are you going along with this? Why do you put up with it? Why do you always put up with everything?!

Kirsch looks at her. Helene gives an angry sob and goes off. Kirsch keeps scrubbing, then pauses, gets up, looks around, looks down at his costume, looks into the auditorium and comes to the front of the stage.

KIRSCH: (*finally able to speak his beloved lines without interruption*) I am a Jew. Hath not a Jew eyes? Hath not a Jew hands, organs, dimensions, senses, affections, passions; fed with the same food, hurt with the same weapons, subject to the same diseases, healed by the same means, warmed and cooled by the same winter and summer, as a Christian is? If you prick us, do we not bleed? If you tickle us, do we not laugh? If you poison us, do we not die? And if you wrong us, shall we not revenge? If we are like you in the rest, we will resemble you in that. If a Jew wrong a Christian, what is his humility? Revenge! If a Christian wrong a Jew, what would his sufferance be by Christian example? Why, revenge! The villainy you teach me I will execute, and it shall go hard but I will better the instruction.

Curtain.

SCENE 3

One year later.

Dim lights in the auditorium. Strassky is leaning against the front of the stage, Polacek sits in a seat in the auditorium.

STRASSKY: (*turning his head to the stage*) Curtain!

The curtain rises. No set, working lights. One or two chairs are scattered about, one downstage at the side. Eder appears from the wings and looks at Strassky.

STRASSKY: Heil Hitler, Herr Eder.

EDER: (*mutters*) Yeah, high hitter. (*Out loud:*) Need anything? Chair, table, lectern?

STRASSKY: No, the gentleman will stand and he doesn't need any props.

Eder turns away.

STRASSKY: Oh, Herr Eder!

Eder turns around.

STRASSKY: A crossbow! Bring down a crossbow!

EDER: A crossbow. Whatever. (*Exits*).

STRASSKY: (*To Polacek, continuing an interrupted conversation*) So they gave me a proper dressing down! For acting according to National Socialist principles! It's incredible! I thought we were finally rid of him and now we're stuck with him again! I just don't get it.

POLACEK: That's what always happens if you fight for a cause, Hubert. You're the one they send in first, you're the one who has to face the enemy fire, and then the cause triumphs and suddenly you're sidelined. The only people who survive every revolution are the bureaucrats. Oh well, at least we're getting to play our dream roles now, that's something.

STRASSKY: I don't care about acting, I never cared.

POLACEK: You're joking.

STRASSKY: No, I'm not. When I hear the word culture, I reach for my revolver. Culture is decadent, effeminate. Every kind of culture, every kind of art. Unnecessary.

Polacek is somewhat taken aback.

POLACEK: Forgive me if this sounds naive, but in that case why did you become an actor?

STRASSKY: (*grins*) Probably because I like making speeches. Because people feel hate on stage, people die. A play with no hatred, no death, bores me rigid. Of course, in that respect old Shakespeare's top notch. There's something Teutonic about him anyway. He's no English dandy. Besides, we Germans can play him better than the English, they don't understand him at all. Much too flabby, a bunch of softies. Like old Kirsch, eh? Wanted to give us a humanitarian Shakespeare. But I showed him, remember? Ran him through – verbally. (*Makes a triumphant gesture with two raised fists.*) You know, I feel great when I get to shout. I love it. But in real life you can't shout at people all the time. If only because of the ladies. Girls always cringe so pathetically, I could kill them. And you're not supposed to shout, of course. So I went into acting. Whatever. – I tell, you I shall honestly be glad when the war comes.

POLACEK: Well, in my case it's a lot less complicated. I'm just an old ham. I love the smell of greasepaint.

In the meantime Morovitz and Meisel come down through the auditorium.

MEISEL: No, please, what are you trying to do to me now, I'm not a, let him go and join an amdram group or something –

STRASSKY: Heil Hitler, Herr Meisel.

MEISEL: Hello Hitler, morning, Heil. For God's sake, Strassky, have you gone completely, is this some kind of, I mean, we're not some village theater, is this your way of rui –, but you're wrong there, you won't get the better of me so ..., wipe that look off your face, Strassky, it won't get you anywhere, I'm still the manager, am I not?

STRASSKY: You're only still here because your accounts are in such a mess that no one else can understand them.

MEISEL: Yes, unfortunately I can't understand them either, what do you think I am, an accountant? Is it my fault if you sack my book-keeper, after thirty years' loyal, just because her husband is a communist railway worker or whatever, what have you got against communist railway workers, Strassky, I knew him, he talked a lot like you, I thought he was a Nazi, but no, now I come to think about it, he never mentioned the Master Race.

STRASSKY: Don't push your luck, Meisel!

MEISEL. Herr Meisel, if you don't mind, I'm still the manager, am I not?

STRASSKY: I'm going to send for the fellow now.

MEISEL: But don't ever try to impose a party comrade on

me again, an absolute amateur, because I've covered my back now, you'll see.

MOROVITZ: You'll be amazed, Herr Meisel. The man is incredible. Really.

MEISEL: (*to Strassky*) Very well, since he's come so, but don't imagine you, I'm the one who decides who to engage here and no one else, where would we all be, the National Socialist state isn't a democracy, thank goodness and Heil.

STRASSKY: (*shouts*) Eder, bring the fellow on. Eder!

EDER'S VOICE: Yeah, yeah, coming.

Kirsch enters. He is dressed like a Tyrolean hill farmer, very convincingly, with a greasy, worn pair of Lederhosen, woollen knee socks, a coarse, collarless linen shirt, a Tyrolean jacket, a hat with a capercaillie feather in it, sturdy hob-nailed boots and a rucksack. His clothes should not be exaggeratedly Tyrolean but look "genuine." He has also grown a long, bushy beard and moustache; the beard and moustache and his hair, which had been dark, have been dyed to make them lighter (as blond as possible without looking ridiculous). In general he makes a very manly, imposing and dignified impression. A Nazi newspaper is sticking out of his pocket. He comes from the side upstage, so that at first only his back can be seen, peers around the stage in astonishment, takes a few steps backwards, turns round, stares into the auditorium, is quite overcome and takes his hat off respectfully. Eder appears upstage, watching.

STRASSKY: Herr Höllrigl!

KIRSCH: (*speaks with a strong rural accent, here rendered as Lowland Scots*) Och, yer aw oot there. [Oh, you're all out there.]

STRASSKY: This is our director and manager, Herr Meisel. You already know the other gentlemen.

KIRSCH: (*Kneels and reaches his hand down to Meisel*) Heil Hitler, guid mornin'. [Heil Hitler, good morning.]

MEISEL: (*reluctantly shakes his hand*) Yes, yes, good morning, Heil.

Kirsch squeezes Meisel's hand very powerfully, Meisel removes his hand with difficulty, shakes it, looks at Kirsch in consternation, suddenly goes to the back of the auditorium, then turns around at the last minute.

MEISEL: I won't put up with this, I'm not here to, if you think you can make a laughing stock, if this is some kind of joke, I'm going to ring the ministry in Berlin now, I'd like to know what they'll –.

MOROVITZ: It's not a joke, Herr Meisel. The fellow's good, he really is good. Just give him a chance.

POLACEK: Nobody's trying to make a laughing stock of you, nobody!

Meisel reconsiders, then comes quickly back to the front of the auditorium and sits down in one of the seats.

MEISEL: (*to Kirsch*) Very well! You can begin! I'm like Atlas here, I've got other things to, hurry up!

POLACEK: But you can't treat him like this, Herr Meisel. He's nervous. You've got to give him time.

MOROVITZ: This is the first time in his life he's ever been on stage.

KIRSCH: (*points at Meisel, looks at Morovitz*) Who's this fellow?

MOROVITZ: That's our director. He runs the theater.

KIRSCH: Aw aye, ah met a bank director once. He wiz a tourist. Ah gave him a drink o' goat's milk, but he threw up. It wiz too rich fur him. [Is he now? I met a bank director once. He was a tourist. I gave him a drink of goat's milk, but he threw up. It was too rich for him.]

POLACEK: I think it would be best if you were to tell the director something about yourself.

KIRSCH: Tell him aboot maself? Wheesht, whit is there tae tell? Ah come frae Tyrol, frae the mountains. Frae Ötztal. Piburg. D'ye ken the area, Herr Meisel? [Tell him about myself? Heavens, what is there to tell? I come from Tyrol, from the mountains. From Ötztal. Piburg. Do you know the area, Herr Meisel?]

Strassky and Morovitz have also sat down.

MEISEL: No, I'm afraid I don't, most regrettable, I suppose you think I should?

KIRSCH: Everyone kens Piburg where ah come frae. But ah dinnae live down in the village, ah'm right up past the screes, even the chickens wear crampons up there. We only come down intae the valley twice a year, once when there's a mudslide and once when there's an avalanche. (*Laughs.*) Nae, nae, it's no really so bad, but ye've got tae be sure-footed. Ah wish ye could see it in summer, and ah'd introduce ye tae our mountain schnapps as well. [Everyone knows Piburg where I come from. But I don't live down in the village, I'm right up past the screes, even the chickens wear crampons up there.

We only come down into the valley twice a year, once when there's a mudslide and once when there's an avalanche. (*Laughs.*) No, no, it's not really so bad, but you've got to be sure-footed. I wish you could see it in summer, and I'd introduce you to our mountain schnapps as well.]

MEISEL: Very kind, but I'm afraid I must decline. Frankly, I don't give a damn about mountains, I don't even like looking at them from below, it makes me dizzy. But I understand the mountain goats are very impressive and those whatchamacallits, those flowers, where everybody tumbles down ravines and so on.

KIRSCH: You dinnae like the mountains? [You don't like the mountains?]

MEISEL: No, I don't give a damn about them. Or about meadows and woods and little animals and things. I find it all distinctly creepy. Nature in general. But you aren't supposed to be asking me questions, I'm the one who's supposed to be listening to you. Tell me, Herr –

KIRSCH: Höllrigl. Benedikt Höllrigl's ma name, like ma da. [Höllrigl. Benedikt Höllrigl's my name, like my father.]

MEISEL: What I should like to know, Herr Höllrigl, is how you, a Tyrolean hill farmer, as I observe, how you hit upon the absurd idea of wanting to become an actor, that really takes the, I simply don't understand it, though I suppose one has to see the humorous side of, please, carry on, do tell me more.

KIRSCH: Wheesht mon, ah jest cannae believe you dinnae like the mountains. [Gosh, I just can't believe you don't like the moutains.]

POLACEK: Herr Höllrigl! Why don't you tell us how this desire to be an actor developed?

KIRSCH: It's fate, so it is. Destiny. I cannae explain it any other way. It's in ma bluid. Ah've goat tae be an actor. (*Holds up the papers that he has in his hand.*) Here are ma papers, ma Roman Catholic baptism certificate, and certificates fur ma da, my ma, ma granny – [It's fate, so it is. Destiny. I can't explain it any other way. It's in my blood. I've got to be an actor. (*Holds up the papers that he has in his hand.*) Here are my papers, my Roman Catholic baptism certificate, and certificates for my father, my mother, my grandmother –]

MEISEL: (*gets up in irritation*) We don't need all that now, Herr Holewiggle.

KIRSCH: Höllrigl, Benedikt Höllrigl.

STRASSKY: There's no need to be touchy, Herr Höllrigl! Just tell us your story!

POLACEK: Why don't you tell us how you learned to read?

KIRSCH: Och, we can aw read, it's no like we're ignorant. But ah must say, we dinnae read a great deal, we've nae time fur it. In winter maybe, it's easier then, but we've nae much to read. It costs money, ye ken. We did huv an almanac, ah read that as a wee laddie. Aye, in winter ah'd read it ten times over till ah kent it by heart. And if anyone wantit tae ken sumhin, like when and where the next cattle market wiz, then ah kent it. And aw the holidays and aw the saints' days, when they were, whit date, whit day o' the week, I kent it aw by heart. [Oh, we can all read, it's not as if we're ignorant. But I must say, we don't read a great deal, we've no time for it. In winter maybe, it's easier then, but we haven't got much to read. It costs money, you know. We did have an almanac, I read that when I was a little boy. Really, in winter I'd read it ten times over till I knew it by heart. And if anyone wanted to know something, like when and where the next cattle market was, then I knew it. And all the holidays and all the saints' days, when they were, what date, what day of the week, I knew it all by heart.]

MEISEL: Fascinating, I must say.

KIRSCH: Aw aye? D'ye think so? [Oh? Do you think so?]

MEISEL: Absolutely fascinating.

KIRSCH: Aw weel, ah'll carry on then. When ah wiz ten, the stable laddie gi' me a book, it was set in Africa. On the front cover wiz a hunter wi' a funny hat, and a blackamoor. I read that in the hay loft, and after that ah kent that the world disnae end over there, beyond yon mountains, because ah'd learnt that somewhere yonder there's another country, called Africa. [Oh well, I'll carry on then. When I was ten, the stable lad gave me a book, it was set in Africa. On the front cover was a hunter with a funny hat, and a blackamoor. I read that in the hay loft, and after that I knew that the world doesn't end over there, beyond those mountains, because I'd learned that somewhere over there there's another country, called Africa.]

MEISEL: You don't say.

KIRSCH: Afterwards ma da caught me in the hay loft and whacked me guid and proper, bled like a stuck pig, so ah did. [Afterwards my father caught me in the hay loft and whacked me good and proper, bled like a stuck pig, so I did.]

POLACEK: But why did he do that?

KIRSCH: Why d'ye think ah hid in the hay loft? It wiznae on account o' the black mon, 'cuz ma da knew aboot them frae the Three Wise Men, one o' them's a blackamoor, he's called Balthasar. Only Balthasar's got posh clothes on, he's a king. The darkie only had a, a kind of pinny on, round here. But that wiznae the reason. Naw, it wiz on account o' the lassie on the front cover, a right bonny lassie wi' golden hair, and no more'n a wee scrap o' clothing oan. Aye, that's how it wiz. Ah kent that book off by heart, and that's how ah learnt tae talk proper, frae reading. [Why do you think I hid in the hay loft? It wasn't on account of the black man, because my father knew about them from the Three Wise Men, one of them's a blackamoor, he's called Balthasar. Only Balthasar's got posh clothes on, he's a king. The darkie only had a, a kind of pinny on, round here. But that wasn't the reason. No, it was on account of the girl on the front cover, a really pretty girl with golden hair, and no more than a little scrap of clothing on. That's how it was. I knew that book off by heart, and that's how I learned to speak properly, from reading.]

MEISEL: You don't say.

KIRSCH: Cuz nae one speaks proper where ah come frae, no even the priest, when he's givin' his sermon. Mon, does he ken how tae preach! But ah dinnae go tae kirk anymore, cuz it diznae agree wi' me. Ah always say God widnae let himself be locked up in a golden tabernacle, God's out in the free air, in nature. These priests turn everything arse forwards. [Because no one speaks properly where I come from, not even the priest, when he's giving his sermon. Boy, does he know how to preach! But I don't go to church anymore, because it doesn't agree with me. I always say God wouldn't let himself be locked up in a golden tabernacle, God's out in the free air, in nature. These priests turn everything arse forwards.]

STRASSKY: You're really something, Höllrigl. I'm impressed.

KIRSCH: Shall ah keep goin'? Weel, ah often bled like a stuck pig, cuz ah kept on reading books, and ma da reckoned ah was gooin' soft in the heid from aw that reading. And it used up too much oil at night and kept me frae working. He wiz right and aw. But ah couldnae help maself, it wiz ma destiny, d'ye see. And when ah wiz fifteen ah startit hitting back and when ah goat tae aboot seventeen he stopped cuz ah dislocated both his shoulders. Mon, but he wiz a scrawny, hunchbacked wee fellow, poor devil. Ah couldnae help likin' him. And he wiz a tough wee bugger, so he wiz. One winter he wiz out chopping firewood and a tree fell on him, he wiz trapped fur five hours in the snow and the freezing cold, four toes on his right foot goat frostbitten, only his big toe wiz left. O' course, it wiz embarrassing, cuz then he kept banging it on things, cuz that one big toe wiz sticking out. So whit he does, he takes his shoe off, he takes his sock off, he lays his foot on the chopping block, picks up his axe and wham! – nae more big toe. Aye, so as ah wiz saying, when ah wiz thirteen the priest gave me some Westerns tae read, no bad, no bad at all, so then ah kent that beyond our mountains there's Kurdistan, right, and Mohammedans and America and Red Indians, so ah learned a lot frae them. Ah still ken them by heart. And afterwards came whit ye might call the turning point, but by then ah wiz thirty and ah'd taken over the farm. They were pitting oan a passion play in Ötz and they said "Benedikt, ye've got tae play Judas." "Aw aye," says I, "ah'll be Judas." And then ah found oot that they'd already asked twenty-five other people tae play Judas. D'ye ken why? [Shall I keep going? Well, I often bled like a stuck pig, because I kept on reading books, and my dad reckoned I was going soft in the head from all that reading. And it used up too much oil at night and kept me from working. He was right and all. But I couldn't help it, it was my destiny, you see. And when I was fifteen I started hitting back and when I got to about seventeen he stopped because I dislocated both his shoulders. Boy, he was a scrawny, hunchbacked little fellow, poor devil. I couldn't help liking him. And he was a tough little bugger, he was. One winter he was out chopping firewood and a tree fell on him, he was trapped for five hours in the snow and the freezing cold, four toes on his right foot got frostbitten, only his big toe was left. Of course, it was embarrassing, because then he kept banging it against things, because that one big toe was sticking out. So what he does, he takes his shoe off, he takes his sock off, he lays his foot on the chopping block, picks up his axe and wham – no more big toe. Well, so as I was saying, when I was thirteen the priest gave me some Westerns to read, not bad, not bad at all, so then I knew that beyond our mountains there's Kurdistan, right, and Mohammedans and America and Red Indians, so I learned a lot from them. I still know them by heart. And afterwards came what you might call the turning point, but by then I was thirty and I'd taken over the farm. They were putting on a passion play in Ötz and they said "Benedikt, you've got to play Judas." "All right," says I, "I'll be Judas." And then I found out that they'd already asked twenty-five other people to play Judas. Do you know why?]

MEISEL: No, not a clue.

KIRSCH: (*Stares at Meisel in amazement*) Why, because he betrayed the Son o' God! – But anyway, ah didnae care, I told maself Judas is a better part than Jesus Christ. Because Jesus Christ jest looks pathetic and talks aw poncey like. Whit kind of a part is that? Boring as hell. But Judas, the traitor, now he's sumhin else, that's a real part fur an actor, eh? [Why, because he betrayed the Son of God! – But anyway, I didn't care, I told myself Judas is a better part than Jesus Christ. Because Jesus Christ just grimaces and talks all stuck-up. What kind of a part is that? Boring as hell. But Judas, the traitor, now he's something else, that's a real part for an actor, eh?]

STRASSKY: Absolutely.

KIRSCH: Right, well, so we rehearse this play – och, it wiz awful, awful! Nae one could act, they jest waved thur arms aboot and shouted, aboot as much feeling as a block o' wood. And then me, with ma gift fur acting, ah wiz like the real Judas, ah WAS Judas! Ah had fiery red hair and a fiery red beard, aw hunchbacked and limping, like the Wandering Jew. And what happened? The audience aw thought ah was the real Judas and beat me up after the first performance. I ended up in hospital. But ah was proud as Punch, ah'm tellin' ye. And five years later came the second turning point. Ah'm walking past the teacher's hoose in Ötz, the old schoolteacher had jest died, and ah see his wife jest about tae set fire tae a whole pile o' books. So ah hop right over the fence, blow oot her match and smack her in the face. Dinnae ye goo burning books, ah says, that's a sin, that is. Dinnae get me wrong, they wiznae Jew books, o' course Jew books should be burnt. Ah mean, ah've no ever read a Jew book, but ah've heard there are terrible things in them, ah read aboot it in the newspaper. What exactly is in these Jew books, dae any of ye ken? [Right, well, so we rehearse this play – gosh, it was awful, awful! No one could act, they just waved their arms about and shouted, about as much feeling as a block of wood. And then me, with my gift for acting, I was like the real Judas, I WAS Judas. I had fiery red hair and a fiery red beard, all hunchbacked and limping, like the Wandering Jew. And what happened? The audience all thought I was the real Judas and beat me up after the first performance. I ended up in hospital. But I was as proud as Punch, I'm telling you. And five years later came the second turning point. I'm walking past the teacher's house in Ötz, the old schoolteacher had just died, and I see his wife just about to set fire to a whole pile of books. So I hop right over the fence, blow out her match and smack her in the face. Don't you go burning books, says I, that's a sin, that is. Don't get me wrong, they weren't Jew books, of course Jew books should be burnt. I mean, I haven't ever read a Jew book, but I've heard there are terrible things in them, I read about it in the newspaper. What exactly is in these Jew books, do any of you know?]

STRASSKY: (*grinning*) Decadent filth, Herr Höllrigl.

KIRSCH: Huh? Whit's that? [Huh? What's that?]

STRASSKY: You'd better ask the director, he used to have a real predilection for that sort of play.

MEISEL: Well, really, Herr Strassky, please don't accuse me –

KIRSCH: Ye pit on Jew plays, dae ye, Herr Meisel? Well, in that case ye willnae catch me acting in this theatre. Because ah dinnae want tae ken aboot this filth and decky-dent stuff, but ah DAE ken that the Jews crucified our Lord and Redeemer, that ah dae ken. Because even if ah dinnae goo tae Chapel, ah willnae hear a word said against our Lord and Redeemer, even if ah didnae want to play him, because it's a lousy part. Naw, naw, if it's like that, then ah'm off. Ah'm sure ah can find another theatre where they dinnae pit oan Jew plays. [You put on Jew plays, do you, Herr Meisel? Well, in that case you won't catch me acting in this theater. Because I don't want to know about this filth and decky-dent stuff, but I DO know that the Jews crucified our Lord and Redeemer, that I do know. Because even if I don't go to church, I won't hear a word said against our Lord and Redeemer, even if I didn't want to play him, because it's a lousy part. No, no, if it's like that, then I'm off. I'm sure I can find another theater where they don't put on Jew plays.]

POLACEK: (*smugly*) But we don't anymore, Herr Höllrigl! Herr Meisel has changed, he's seen the error of his ways and of course he doesn't put on Jewish plays anymore.

STRASSKY: Don't worry, Herr Höllrigl. The age of decadence is over.

KIRSCH: Aye, weel, ah should bluidy well hope that that decky-wotsit –. Aw right then, ah'll stay. Where had ah got tae? [Yes, well, I should bloody well hope that that decky-whatsit –. All right then, I'll stay. Where had I got to?]

MOROVITZ: The teacher's books.

KIRSCH: That's right. So ah smack her in the heid, the widow, and ah say "Ye gi' me those books right now, ye wicked wumin." She goes straight off intae the house wi' her face aw swollen and locks the door, ah stick the books in ma rucksack – but ah left her a wee bit o' sugar and flour, since her face wiz so swollen up, cuz when ah hit someone, they stay hit – and I heid out fur the forest, unpack them and take a closer look. They were aw plays, nothing but theatre plays. So ah startit tae read, and ah read and ah read until the sun went down. Weel, a whole new world opened up fur me! Friedrich Schiller, Johann Wolfgang von Goethe, Heinrich von Kleist, that fellow wi' the foreign name... (*Suddenly horrified.*) Bluidy hell, ah read one book about a Jew. "The Merchant of Venice". Wiz he a Jew then, that writer? [That's right. So I smack her in the head, the widow, and I say "You give me those books right now, you wicked woman." She goes straight off into the house with her face all swollen and locks the door, I stick the books in my rucksack – but I left her a little bit of sugar and flour, as her face was so swollen up, because when I hit someone, they stay hit – and I head out for the forest, unpack them and take a closer look. They were all plays, nothing but theater plays. So I started to read, and I read and I read until the sun went down. Well, a whole new world opened up for me! Friedrich Schiller, Johann Wolfgang von Goethe, Heinrich von Kleist, that fellow with the foreign name... (*Suddenly horrified*.) Bloody hell, I read one book about a Jew. "The Merchant of Venice." Was he a Jew then, that writer?]

STRASSKY: But of course not, Herr Höllrigl. That's Shakespeare, good old Shakespeare.

KIRSCH: Whew, that's a relief, he wrote some bluidy guid plays aboot battles and things. But tae get back tae me, over the winter ah read aw those plays, and ah read them again and again, until ah kent them off by heart. So then ah thought, ye cannae keep this to yerself, ye've got tae let other people know, these could really teach 'em sumhin. At first ah used to read them out at home in the evenings. Ma da wiz still alive then, they used tae make him weep, but it wiznae cuz he liked the plays, it wiz cuz he wanted tae smack me one, but he wiz too auld by then. My wife used to cry too, cuz she thought ah wiz goin' mad, my ma wid fall asleep and ma weans laughed at me behind ma back. So ah started going tae Chapel again and after Mass ah'd recite the plays in front o' the Chapel. But not fur long, because either everyone laughed at me, or they spat on ma feet – "That's nae way fur a farmer tae behave," ye ken how it is – and they even wanted to pit me in a lunatic asylum, can ye imagine! Well, the years passed, ah kept sneaking off tae town, tae Imst, and bought maself new books, ma da died, my ma died, ma wife died, an avalanche got two of ma weans, one of ma lassies jumped intae the river cuz ah scolded her a bit on account of her having a basturt bairn, ma eldest lad's got the farm, ah handed it over tae him a week ago, and now ah'm here and ah want tae act. [Whew, that's a relief, he wrote some bloody good plays about battles and things. But to get back to me, over the winter I read all those plays, and I read them again and again, until I knew them off by heart. So then I thought, you can't keep this to yourself, you've got to let other people know, these could really teach them something. At first I used to read them out at home in the evenings. My dad was still alive then, they used to make him weep, but it wasn't because he liked the plays, it was because he wanted to smack me one, but he was too old by then. My wife used to cry too, because she thought I was going mad, my mother would fall asleep and my children laughed at me behind my back. So I started going to church again and after Mass I'd recite the plays in front of the church. But not for long, because either everyone laughed at me, or they spat on my feet – "That's no way for a farmer to behave," you know how it is – and they even wanted to put me in a lunatic asylum, can you imagine! Well, the years passed, I kept sneaking off to town, to Imst, and bought myself new books, my dad died, my mother died, my wife died, an avalanche got two of my children, one of my daughters jumped into the river because I scolded her a bit on account of her having a bastard child, the eldest boy's got the farm, I handed it over to him a week ago, and now I'm here and I want to act.]

MEISEL: But why in my theater, of all places?
KIRSCH: Weel, because ah'd heard this is a guid theatre. Ah've got tae start somewhere. [Well, because I'd heard this is a good theatre. I've got to start somewhere.]

MEISEL: Very well, you shall have the chance, (*sits down*) really, I've never seen such a, but very well, perform something for us, please begin. What'll it be?

KIRSCH: Ah can recite a whole play fur ye. [I can recite a whole play for you.]

MEISEL: (*imploringly*) No, please don't! Do a monologue! Only not a long one, I couldn't endure, God, what have I done to deserve this?

STRASSKY: Eder! The crossbow!

Eder exits.

KIRSCH: Ah, guid. That's jest the thing. [Ah, good. That's just the thing.]

Eder comes back with a crossbow, gives it to Kirsch, looks at him in irritation, then goes upstage, leans against something and watches. Kirsch puts his papers in his pocket, puts his hat down and goes off into the wings.

MEISEL: Come on, get on with it, Herr Holewiggle!

Kirsch enters and comes downstage. He gives a magnificent performance as Tell, with scarcely a trace of dialect in his speech (that is to say his accent gradually disappears as he progresses through the monologue).

KIRSCH: Through this ravine he needs must come. There is
No other way to Küssnacht. Here I'll do it!
The ground is everything I could desire.
Yon elder bush will hide me from his view,
And from that point my shaft is sure to hit.
The gorge's narrowness forbids pursuit.

Now, Gessler, balance thine account with heaven!
Thou must away from earth, thy sand is run.
Quiet and harmless was the life I led,
My bow was bent on forest game alone;
No thoughts of murder weighed upon my soul.
But thou hast scared me from my dream of peace;
The milk of human kindness thou hast turn'd
To rankling poison in my breast, and made
Appalling deeds familiar to my soul.
He who could make his own child's head his mark
Can speed his arrow to his foeman's heart.
My boys, poor innocents, my loyal wife
Must be protected, tyrant, from thy rage!
When last I drew my bow – with trembling hand –
And thou, with fiendishly remorseless glee,
Forced me to level at my own child's head,
When I, imploring pity, writhed before thee,
Then, in the anguish of my soul, I vow'd
A fearful oath, which met God's ear alone,
That when my bow next wing'd an arrow's flight
Its aim should be thy heart. The vow I made,
Amid the hellish torments of that moment,
I hold a sacred debt, and I will pay it.
    (IV,3; Tr. Theodore Martin, Project Gutenberg E-text 2782)

MEISEL: (*gets up*) Thank you, that will suffice.

KIRSCH: Thou art my lord, my Emperor's delegate –

MEISEL: (*interrupting*) I said, that's enough!
Strassky, Polacek and Morovitz applaud and get up.

STRASSKY: (*to Meisel*) Why did you interrupt?

MEISEL: I don't like *William Tell*, I just don't like it, it gives me a head– , I'm sorry, I just find it (*takes a pill*), this classical stuff, this puffed up, no, I won't have *William Tell* on my stage!

STRASSKY: Just tell me one thing, Herr Meisel. How was he? (*Points at Kirsch.*)

MEISEL: Good, good, the fellow is astonishingly good, he's clearly got a gift, didn't disgrace himself by any means, no, really astonishing, whatever next. I remember! Edelweiss, Herr Holewiggle, that's what the thingamajig's called, Edelweiss.

KIRSCH: Ye, Herr Meisel, ye'd better watch it or ah'll come doon off this stage and smack ye in the heid! Whit did ye call Tell? Puffed up is he? I cannae –, but you, you should be locked up, so ye should! Calls himself a theatre director in our glorious German Reich and says Tell is puffed up! When it wiz written by one of our greatest German poets, Friedrich Schiller! (*To Strassky:*) And ye pit up wi' it? [You, Herr Meisel, you'd better watch it or I'll come down off this stage and smack you in the head! What did you call Tell? Puffed up is he? I can't –, but you, you should be locked up, so you should! Calls himself a theater director in our glorious German Reich and says Tell is puffed up! When it was written by one of our greatest German poets, Friedrich Schiller! (*To Strassky:*) And you put up with it?]

STRASSKY: Not for much longer, Herr Höllrigl, not for much longer. (*To Meisel:*) Well, what do you think? Will you take him on or not?

MEISEL: (*despairingly*) And what parts would he play?

STRASSKY: Why, William Tell, of course, what else?

MEISEL: Over my dead – (*Searches desperately for arguments*) He isn't qualified, he hasn't had any training, he's not allowed to act without, that would contravene the, where would we be if everyone...?

KIRSCH: Och, ma performer's licence, ah've goat that as well! (*Fishes for a piece of paper and holds it up.*) [Oh, my performer's licence, I've got that as well!]

STRASSKY: We sorted out his authorization this morning, Herr Meisel.

MOROVITZ: Herr Meisel! I don't understand what's eating you! We'll have a full house every night! This will be a sensation! A Tyrolean farmer as star actor!

KIRSCH: Right, ah'm off. Ah ken when ah'm no wanted. (*Exiting.*) There are plenty of other theatres. [Right, I'm off. I know when I'm not wanted. (*Exiting.*) There are plenty of other theaters.]

STRASSKY: (*hisses at Meisel*) The second Herr Höllrigl leaves this stage you are out of a job, I swear it.

MEISEL: Herr Höllrigl!

KIRSCH: (*has already gone off, comes two steps back*) Whit is it? [What is it?]

MEISEL: I give in, I yield to, as of now you are a member of this ensemble.

KIRSCH: Whit's the pay? Because ah'm no actin' fur peanuts,

that's fur sure. [What's the pay? Because I'm not acting for peanuts, that's for sure.]

MEISEL: I couldn't care less, you can come to some agreement with your friends here, at any rate I shall complain to the ministry, because this really won't do! (*Exiting through the auditorium.*) And they call this a dictatorship, everyone does what he likes, funny kind of dictatorship, a dictatorship of philistines, that's what it is, Heil and good day, I've had it up to here with, no really.

STRASSKY: Well, we did it! This calls for a celebration.

KIRSCH: Ah'd be glad of a dram. Ma throat's a wee bit dry. [I'd be glad of a drink. My throat's a bit dry.]

Strassky, Morovitz and Polacek climb onto the stage. Strassky puts his arm around Kirsch's shoulder.

STRASSKY: Eder!

Eder comes on. Strassky takes Kirsch's crossbow and throws it to him, Eder catches it reluctantly.

KIRSCH: (*to Eder*) We've no yet bin introduced, have we? Ah wiz a wee bit worked up. Ah'm Benedikt Höllrigl, actor. (*Shakes him by the hand.*) Ah'm gooin' tae be acting in plays. And who might ye be? [We haven't been introduced yet, have we? I was a bit worked up. I'm Benedikt Höllrigl, actor. (*Shakes him by the hand.*) I'm going to be acting in plays. And who might you be?]

EDER: I'm the stage manager. (*Coldly:*) But Herr Strassky is kind enough to use me as props manager, odd jobs man and curtain puller as well.

KIRSCH: Who would huv thought there'd be so many people in a theatre. D'ye really need aw o' them? We didnae need aw that when we did our passion play. [Who would have thought there'd be so many people in a theater. Do you really need all of them? We didn't need all that when we did our passion play.]

EDER: D'you want to see me out of a job, Herr Höllrigl?

KIRSCH: Nae, o' course not, ah'm sure it's aw right and proper, ah dinnae ken much aboot the professional theatre yet. Main thing is, ye're no' decadent, right? (*Pats him on the arm.*) We're going tae get along, Heil Hitler, see ye around. [No, of course not, I'm sure it's all right and proper, I don't know much about the professional theater yet. Main thing is, you're not decadent, right? (*Pats him on the arm.*) We're going to get along, Heil Hitler, see you around.]

Kirsch exits with Strassky, Morovitz and Polacek. Eder stares after them in astonishment. He has recognized Kirsch but is still not quite certain. Blackout.

SCENE 4

Working lights on stage, no set. Eder is in the same position, waiting for someone. Kirsch enters in his Tyrolean costume, with his rucksack, but without his hat. They look at one other.

EDER: It is you, ain't it?

KIRSCH: Yes, it's me.
EDER: I couldn't sleep all night. I can't believe it! It's impossible!

KIRSCH: Did you recognize me straight away, Herr Eder? That would be very disappointing.

EDER: Of course not, not straight away. It's an amazingly good act. But you know I've got good ears. When you started sounding off, I thought, here, I know that voice! – (*Unable to contain himself:*) It's insane! What the hell d'you think you're up to, Herr Kirsch?! (*Starts in horror, because he has spoken his name out loud, looks around and lowers his voice.*) What are you playing at? You know you're risking your life?

KIRSCH: Yes, I know.

EDER: Yeah, well, so why are you doing it, then?

KIRSCH: I've got to act. If I can't act as a Jew then I'll act as an Aryan. Right?

EDER: But you'll never get away with it! You can't act a part in real life!

KIRSCH: Why not? People have done it – what about the Captain from Köpenick, the fellow who dressed up as an army officer and took over a whole town? He existed in real life as well as in Zuckmayer's play, you know.

EDER: But he was wearing a uniform! That's different! If you've got a uniform on then that's all people see!

KIRSCH: True, but isn't that just what I'm doing? Look at me. I'm wearing a beard, I'm wearing Tyrolean lederhosen, so I must be a Tyrolean peasant. And everyone believes me. Except for you. (*Scottish accent:*) But it's no everyone who's got yer ears, Herr Eder. [But not everyone's got your ears, Herr Eder.]

EDER: But other people are gonna recognize you as well. Like your wife. Well, okay, so of course she won't betray you, but – it'll get around, people've got eyes in their heads.

KIRSCH: Have they?

EDER: (*shakes his head*) I'm gobsmacked. How could you, no, I'd never've believed it, you of all people! (*Shakes his head.*) Where did you learn to speak the dialect like that?

KIRSCH: In Piburg. From Farmer Höllrigl. Where else?

EDER: So he really exists?

KIRSCH: Of course he does.

EDER: Okay – so how'd you find him, then?

KIRSCH: I wanted to cross the mountain border at Ötztal, with the children, secretly, at night. But we got lost as soon as we'd entered the valley and ended up by a rockfall somewhere. We nearly fell down it in the dark. It was raining terribly. The children were crying, they wanted to go back... Suddenly we saw light from a lantern. We crept into the bushes, I thought maybe it was the border guards. But it was only a farmer. I was so desperate I called out to him, even though I knew he might betray us. But he didn't betray us. They took us in like old friends. His mother took care of the children and put them to bed ... and then Benedikt offered to take us across the Swiss border the following night. So there we are, sitting in his kitchen, drinking schnapps, and Benedikt's telling stories, he's a wonderful storyteller, and I'm looking at his great big bushy beard and his lederhosen – and suddenly I get this crazy idea. Benedikt was delighted, absolutely delighted. We were both completely drunk and I'd forgotten all about it the next morning, but Benedikt hadn't forgotten at all and he was still delighted with the idea. – I stayed with them for a whole year. The children and I helped work in the fields, I grew a beard and learned the local dialect. Then Benedikt gave me his clothes and his identity papers, and here I am.

EDER: This is gonna end badly, I can feel it in my bones.

KIRSCH: Herr Eder! At least if I go, I'll go out with a bang. Not like last time. Or do you want me to just turn the other cheek? No! "The villainy you teach me I will execute, and it shall go hard but I will better the instruction."

Strassky comes on stage. He has heard the last line.

STRASSKY: Oh, come on now, Herr Höllrigl! I'm convinced you can play any part you want, but I can't buy you as Shylock! Forget it!

Eder disappears.

KIRSCH: Aye, but that's a cracker of a play, ye've jest got to play it right. Ah'd enjoy playing Shylock, ye know, ah'd make him really unsympathetic, really venomous. [Oh but that's a great play, you've just got to act it right. I'd enjoy playing Shylock, you know, I'd make him really unsympathetic, really venomous.]

Kirsch digs his nails into Strassky's chest over his heart, Strassky gasps for breath and sinks to his knees.
KIRSCH: A pound of flesh, nearest the heart! – Eh?

Kirsch lets go, Strassky totters backwards holding both hands over his heart and looks at Kirsch almost in fear.

STRASSKY: Yes, well, at least you've got the necessary brutality for Shylock, but even so, it would be absurd to have you, the archetypal Aryan, playing the archetypal Jew!

KIRSCH: Och, yer right. Look, Hubert, ah've been waitin' ages. Are ye always this late for rehearsals? It said ten oan the schedule. [Oh, you're right. Look Hubert, I've been waiting ages. Are you always this late for rehearsals? It said ten on the schedule.]

STRASSKY: (*Looks at his watch*) Yes, well, it's quarter past.

KIRSCH: (*Pulls out a pocket watch, looks at it*) Nearly half past. Ah dinnae like this, ah must say. If ah turned up this late for the milking ma cows wid kick up a grand fuss. Two minutes late and they're pissed off. [Nearly half past. I don't like this, I must say. If I turned up this late for the milking, my cows would kick up a huge fuss. Two minutes late and they're annoyed.]

STRASSKY: (*shamefacedly*) They'll be in the canteen, I'll go and get them. (*Exits.*)

Kirsch takes off his rucksack, pulls out his copy of "William Tell," sits down on a chair right at the front of the stage and studies the text intensely.
Helene and Morovitz enter (with their texts), they don't notice Kirsch.
Helene glances round, pulls Morovitz to her and kisses him passionately, the attack takes him by surprise and he is rather embarrassed.

MOROVITZ: Helene, please, not here!

HELENE: (*Steps back*) You don't love me anymore.

MOROVITZ: Of course I –

HELENE: You don't love me any more! You're tired of me! Oh, how quickly you men tire of a woman!

MOROVITZ: But Helene –

HELENE: I showed you my feelings too soon, didn't I? Should I have played games with you instead? Should I? Should I have kept you guessing? I will if you like, I'm good at that, I'm very good at that, I like playing games with men, I always play games with men! (*Shouts at him:*) Do you have any idea who I am, who it is you're dealing with? People send me buckets! Buckets! Buckets full of letters! Fan letters! Love letters! Passionate love letters!

MOROVITZ: But Helene, I –

HELENE: They all love me! They all worship me! They all dream of me! They all want fan photos and autographs! They all want to marry me! And you, you humiliate me!

MOROVITZ: But Helene, that's –

HELENE: (*slaps his cheek*) Don't think you can pull the wool over my eyes! I saw you both, in the café opposite!

MOROVITZ: Who did you –

HELENE: That cow-eyed starlet! I saw her ogling you with her big cow eyes, the stupid cow!

MOROVITZ: Who exactly do you mean, may I ask?

HELENE: I mean Miss Olga! Fräulein Olga Sternberg! She'd

like to play my parts and she'd like to steal my lover! But you won't two-time me, not you, you're still too wet behind the ears! If anyone does any cheating, it'll be me, young man! Don't you forget it!

MOROVITZ: I know THAT, you hardly need to tell me that. The whole town knew how you cheated on your husband and who with. He was the only one who didn't, he was too good-natured, the fool.

HELENE: (*slaps his cheek*) This is outrageous! How dare you call my husband a fool! He was ten times the man you'll ever be!

MOROVITZ: But you still made a cuckold of him. Oh damn, why do we have to quarrel?

HELENE: (*weeping*) Because you don't love me! Because you don't love me! Because you're ashamed to be seen with me! How often do we go out? How often do we go out? You're ashamed to be seen with me! You're ashamed to be seen with such an old hag!

MOROVITZ: Oh stop it! It's not my fault if you're constantly away shooting!

HELENE: (*weeping*) You fancy that cow-eyed slut more than me! That's what it is!

MOROVITZ: We were just talking, Helene! She's got problems! She was just telling me her problems!

HELENE: Oh yes, I know that old trick! I know it really well! Do you think I haven't used it myself? Why doesn't she pull something else out of her bag of tricks? Like her youth?

She could do that, couldn't she?

MOROVITZ: (*shouts at her*) Stop it, all right?! That's enough!

HELENE: (*flings herself sobbing around his neck*) I need you, Gernot, I need you so badly! I've got no one else! No one at all!

MOROVITZ: All right, all right, calm down.–

Polacek, Strassky, Olga and the prompter enter (with their texts). Helene and Morovitz jump apart. Helene turns away and comes downstage (towards Kirsch), secretly wiping away her tears. Kirsch looks at her calmly, she sees him, is startled and turns away from him.

STRASSKY: (*as he enters, to Olga*) Yes, I'm sorry, Olga, it's not my idea, you know that, but – orders are orders.

OLGA: It's going to take a while, Hubert! I'm an illegitimate child! I thought it was only under the old social order that that was considered a disgrace!

STRASSKY: Of course it's not a disgrace anymore! Do you think we're the Moral Majority or something? That's not the point! You need an Aryan pass! No proof of Aryan racial purity, no job! Kindly take note of that!

MOROVITZ: But what's she supposed to do, Hubert? Her mother died without telling her who her father is! She's got everything she needs for her mother's side of the family, I've seen the documents myself!

Helene sees that her jealousy was justified and is offended.

STRASSKY: That's not good enough! Don't you start as well!

(*To Olga:*) You've got another month, okay?

Meisel enters.

MEISEL: Very well! "William Tell!" Where is our leading man?

STRASSKY: He was just –

KIRSCH: Here!

All look at Kirsch. Morovitz is unpleasantly surprised and looks at Helene. Kirsch gets up and comes over to them.

STRASSKY: May I introduce Benedikt Höllrigl, hill farmer and actor. We're very proud …

MEISEL: Yes, well –

STRASSKY: …that as of today Herr Höllrigl is a member of our ensemble.

KIRSCH: Guid day to ye. [Good morning.]

Eder appears upstage and watches with tense curiosity.

STRASSKY: Herr Hö– uh, Benedikt, may I present the grande dame of our theater, Frau Helene Schwaiger (*points at her*), whom you may know from the cinema.

KIRSCH: Nae, I dinnae ken the lady. I dinnae goo tae fillums, the pictures move too fast for me. It gi's me a heid-ache. But even so, guid day, it's an honour for me tae be acting wi' sich a bonny, elegant lady. [No, I don't know the lady. I don't go to films, the pictures move too fast for me. It gives me a headache. But even so, good morning, it's an honor for me to be acting with such a beautiful, elegant lady.]

He goes up to her with outstretched hand, she steps back to avoid him.
HELENE: I won't put up with this! Herr Meisel, I will not put up with this!

Meisel stares at her uncomprehendingly.

HELENE: I refuse to act with a yokel, a peasant! Who do you think I am? (*To Kirsch:*) I don't mean to insult you, Herr Höllrigl, this has nothing to do with you personally! In a film – any time! I often act in films with talented amateurs, I mean, when we need someone to play a little man from the village – peasants, shepherds, artisans – they can be wonderful! But the theater! The theater! That is the highest art form and the most challenging! It's not enough to have an interesting, weather-beaten face! Theatre is about language! About expression! – If you make me act with this man, Herr Meisel, then you can have my resignation here and now! You know I only have to go to the nearest theater and they would plead with me on bended knee to work for them!

MEISEL: Don't tell me all this, Frau Schwaiger, tell your party comrades here, they're the ones who must, must …, not me!

MOROVITZ: Don't be so prejudiced, Helene! The man's a genius! Just look at him! He IS William Tell!

KIRSCH: Wait jest a wee minute, ye stuck-up bissum, ye, wi' your painted face! Jest who do ye think ye are? Ah live for the theatre! Ah wiz born for the theatre! That's all ah've ever cared about! That's why I left ma mountains, that ah miss every single day, that's why ah left ma homeland Tyrol, that means everything tae me, and exchanged it for the big city, where I'm always afraid, afraid o' the crowds, afraid o' the cars, where I get heidaches frae the noise and the stink, where I dinnae ken a soul, where nae one says hello, where there's nae grass and nae cows and nae decent schnapps! And do ye think ye're goin' tae stop me now, when ah've gone through aw that, for jest one thing: tae be an actor, tae show people sumhin, tae teach them sumhin, but not so that they'd notice, jest helpin' them on a wee bit wi' guid plays! This is holy work that we're doing, wumin, and the theatre is a temple and ah'll no' let maself be driven oot o' that temple! D'ye understand me, wumin? [Wait just a minute, you stuck-up hussy, you with your painted face! Just who do you think you are? I live for the theater! I was born for the theater! That's all I've ever cared about! That's why I left my mountains, that I miss every single day, that's why I left my homeland Tyrol, that means everything to me, and exchanged it for the big city, where I'm always afraid, afraid of the crowds, afraid of the cars, where I get headaches from the noise and the stink, where I don't know a soul, where no one says hello, where there's no grass and no cows and no decent schnapps! And do you think you're going to stop me now, when I've gone through all that, for just one thing: to be an actor, to show people something, to teach them something, but not so that they'd notice, just helping them on a bit with good plays! This is holy work that we're doing, woman, and the theater is a temple and I'll not let myself be driven out of that temple! Do you understand me, woman?]

Helene is completely overwhelmed, she goes over to Kirsch and embraces him.
HELENE: Oh, my dear man! Oh, you good soul! What an injustice I've done to you! (*Steps back, looks at him.*) You're burning with passion! Aflame! Oh, I've always longed for this! How I've yearned for it! At long last, an actor with some fire

to him! Herr Meisel, it will be an honor to work with this man!

MEISEL: Well, what a relief.

KIRSCH: Forgive me, Frau Schwaiger, ah may have been a wee bit intense back there. [Forgive me, Frau Schwaiger, I may have been a little bit intense back there.]

HELENE: Wonderful! Wonderful! I love outbursts like that, that are truly heartfelt, I love it!

STRASSKY: May I also introduce Fräulein Olga Sternberg.

KIRSCH: (*shakes her hand*) Guid day, miss.[Good morning, miss.]

STRASSKY: And Frau Jabinger, our prompter.

KIRSCH: (*shakes her hand*) Guid day. [Good morning.] (*To the others:*) WHIT does she do? [WHAT does she do?]

The prompter gives an awestruck curtsey.

MOROVITZ: That's our prompter. She sits in the prompt-box during the performances, in case anyone gets into difficulties.

Kirsch stares in astonishment at the prompt-box.

POLACEK: She prompts us, Herr Höllrigl, if anybody forgets their lines.

KIRSCH: Whit, ye need someone to tell ye yer lines? Do ye no learn the plays by heart? [What, you need someone to tell you your lines? Don't you learn the plays by heart?]

POLACEK: Yes, of course. It's just – every now and then it can happen that someone –

KIRSCH: (*to Helene*) Diz that happen tae ye too, Frau Schwaiger? [Does that happen to you too, Frau Schwaiger?]

HELENE: Certainly not!

KIRSCH: Aye, ah reckon we two are the only ones with any fire to us around here, are we no, Frau Schwaiger? [Yes, I reckon we two are the only ones with any fire to us around here, isn't that right, Frau Schwaiger?]

HELENE: You can bet your bottom dollar on it!

Olga is annoyed.

MEISEL: So, ladies and gentlemen, if I might ask you to, ah yes, there's been a spot of recasting, Frau Schwaiger, you won't be playing Gertrud, you're now Hedwig, Tell's wife.

HELENE: (*offended*) What?

MEISEL: Sorry, but your film commitments...

HELENE: Authorized by the ministry!

MEISEL: ...leave me no choice but to –

HELENE: But Hedwig's a doormat, a supporting role, she doesn't come on until the third act!

MEISEL: Well, my dear Frau Schwaiger, at some point you

will have to, one or the other, you're permanently unavailable, Gertrud has to be rehearsed, this isn't an opera, you can't just plonk yourself anywhere you like on stage, it's hardly fair to your colleagues, there you go sounding off about your love for the theater, how you "burn with passion" for it, but unfortunately I don't see much, you seem to prefer smouldering on screen!

HELENE: I think that's very unfair, Herr Meisel! Dr. Goebbels suggested me personally for this film role, so I could hardly say no! At least let me play Berta, the heiress!

MEISEL: Fräulein Olga will be playing Berta, and I hope you won't try to deprive her of the part, after all, Fräulein Sternberg has refused a number of film offers.

HELENE: Oh really, so she's had offers, has she?

KIRSCH: Frau Schwaiger, ah've got to huv a word wi' ye! Hedwig may no be a grand part, but she's Tell's wife. She's a loving wife and mother! That's important! Verra important! Who's playing her father, Walter Fürst? [Frau Schwaiger, I've got to have a word with you! Hedwig may not be a grand part, but she's Tell's wife. She's a loving wife and mother! That's important! Very important! Who's playing her father, Walter Fürst?]

POLACEK: Yours truly.

Kirsch looks at him, looks at Helene, takes Polacek by the arm, leads him over to Helene and stands him next to her, then steps back and studies the two of them.

KIRSCH: Noo that is a problem. [Now that is a problem.]

MEISEL: What, if I may ask?

KIRSCH: She's too auld. [She's too old.]

MEISEL: I'm sorry, I don't –

KIRSCH: Aye, look at the pair o' them! Frau Schwaiger cannae possibly be Herr Polacek's daughter! [Just look at the pair of them! Frau Schwaiger can't possibly be Herr Polacek's daughter!]

Eder grins in the background, Strassky has to grin too. Olga is also rather pleased.

HELENE: Well, really...!

MEISEL: This is a theater, Herr Holewiggle, not real life!

KIRSCH: Och weel, if we dinnae light her face up too much (*looks up*) wi' those lights (*examines Helene's face critically from the side*) and slap on plenty o' make-up..., aye, aw right, what dae I care, she can play ma wife. [Oh well, if we don't light her face up too much (*looks up*) with those lights (*examines Helene's face critically from the side*) and slap on plenty of make-up..., yes, all right, what do I care, she can play my wife.]

Helene struggles against her tears but has to turn away.

KIRSCH: Ye must forgive me, Frau Schwaiger, if I – . Ye see, in the mountains, where ah come frae, no wumin tries tae make hersel' younger than she is. Why should she? Every age has its beauty. Ma wife wiz always dear tae me. Always. The older we goat, the both of us, the dearer she wiz tae me. To me she jest kept gettin' bonnier and bonnier. Aye, so she did. [You must forgive me, Frau Schwaiger, if I – . You see, in the mountains, where I come from, no woman tries to make herself younger than she is. Why should she? Every age has its beauty. My wife was always dear to me. Always. The older both of us got, the dearer she was to me. To me she just kept getting more and more beautiful. Really she did.]

Polacek starts to move away from Helene.

KIRSCH: Jest a wee moment, Herr Polacek. Jest stay there, would ye? [Just a moment, Herr Polacek. Just stay there, would you?]

Polacek stops and looks at Kirsch in astonishment, Kirsch goes up to him and stares into his face, examines him from the side, runs his hand over his nose and turns to Meisel.

KIRSCH: But HE'S a real problem.

Polacek looks astonished.

MEISEL: Well, I wonder what I'm actually doing here. I'm supposed to be the theater manager, I'm supposed to be the director, that's what it says in my contract, that's what I get paid for – (*shouts despairingly*:) but no one lets me! No one lets me! What is it now, Herr Holewiggle, what infelicity is troubling your alpine soul now?

KIRSCH: Well, ah'm sorry, but d'ye no see it? (*Points at Polacek.*) D'ye really no see it? [Well, I'm sorry, but can't you see it? (*Points at Polacek.*) Can you really not see it?]

MEISEL: What? What, my dear man?

KIRSCH: (*after an impressively dramatic pause*) He looks like a Jew.

General astonishment. Everyone looks at Polacek, who feels uncomfortable and touches his face in embarrassment.

KIRSCH: Does he or does he no? Look at his profile! Ah've goat a book at hame wi' aw the different racial types, aw the faces! A scientific book! Aye, he'd be better for Shylock, better then me, that right, Hubert? [Does he or doesn't he? Look at his profile! I've got a book at home with all the different racial types, all the faces! A scientific book! Really, he'd be better for Shylock, better than me, that right, Hubert?]

STRASSKY: (*suddenly starts to laugh*) He's played him, he's played him!

KIRSCH: That's whit ah'm saying! [That's what I'm saying!]

MOROVITZ: (*also starts to laugh*) He's found you out, hasn't he, Polacek?

POLACEK: (*stuttering*) I got my Aryan pass ages ago!

KIRSCH: Aye, but who knows! Any crook can fake a certificate, believe me, there are whole workshops oot there making counterfeits! [Yes, but who knows! Any crook can fake a certificate, believe me, there are whole workshops out there making counterfeits!]

POLACEK: I swear I'm not a Jew! Honestly!

KIRSCH: Look here, Herr Polacek – hey! Polacek! Whit kind o' a name is that? Polacek! [Look here, Herr Polacek – hey! Polacek! What kind of a name is that? Polacek!]

POLACEK: (*stuttering*) It's a Czech name, Herr Höllrigl!

KIRSCH: So it's a Slav name, right? The Jews aren't the only sub-humans, are they, there are other inferior races as well, are there no? But it's aw the same tae me, we cannae prove anything, Polacek, it's enough that ye look like a Jew. [So it's a Slav name, right? The Jews aren't the only sub-humans, are they, there are other inferior races as well, aren't there? But it's all the same to me, we can't prove anything, Polacek, it's enough that you look like a Jew.]

MOROVITZ: Hang on a minute, now you're taking things a bit too far, Herr Höllrigl!

KIRSCH: Ah'm no' takin' anything too far! Yer obviously not up-tae-date. Ye should read a wee bit more, keep yerselves informed. The representative appointed by the Führer to oversee the entire intellectual and ideological schooling and education of the National Socialist German Workers' Party: who is he? (*Looks about him*) Weel, who is he? [I'm not taking anything too far! You're obviously not up-to-date. You should do a bit more reading, keep yourselves informed. The representative appointed by the Führer to oversee the entire intellectual and ideological education of the National Socialist German Workers' Party: who is he? (*Looks about him*) Well, who is he?]

No one knows. Strassky and Morovitz hang their heads like schoolboys being scolded. Meisel suddenly recognizes Kirsch, stares at him in astonishment, then manages to hide his feelings.

KIRSCH: Rosenberg! Alfred Rosenberg! Stay behind after school, gentlemen! And whit did Rosenberg say? Eh? [Rosenberg! Alfred Rosenberg! Stay behind after school, gentlemen! And what did Rosenberg say? Eh?]

Strassky and Morovitz shrug.

KIRSCH: "I am appalled by the un-Aryan appearance of certain of our well-known German actors! The Ministry of Culture considers it inappropriate that actors with such an unfortunate physiognomy should look down from cinema and theater billboards! Such billboards have the effect of corrupting the racial instinct of the German people and furthermore convey the impression that no progress has been made in ridding German cultural life of Jewish influences!" See, it's no only plays ah ken by heart! Ye cannae fool me! (*To Polacek:*) I thought ye looked suspicious, right frae the start! [See, it's not only plays I know by heart! You can't fool me! (*To Polacek:*) I thought you looked suspicious, right from the start!]

POLACEK: (*terrified*) Herr Höllrigl, please!

KIRSCH: Ye thought ye'd be safe if ye disguised yersel' as a Nazi frae the word go, did ye? Well, ye made a mistake there! Because now ah'm here! Herr Meisel, ah demand that ye dismiss Herr Polacek here and now! [You thought you'd be safe if you disguised yourself as a Nazi from the word go, did you? Well, you made a mistake there! Because now I'm here! Herr Meisel, I demand that you dismiss Herr Polacek here and now!]

MEISEL: But Herr Höllrigl, I can't do that, I find that most improper, I mean (*goes up to Polacek, stares at his face*), well, yes, now that I come to look at him, yes, indeed, you certainly have a point. But it's not that bad, I mean really, on stage one could, with heavy make-up, don't you think? His profile, though, Polacek, your profile is a disaster.

Polacek covers his face with his hands, cringing with shame.

STRASSKY: I have to say, Benedikt, that if we're going to be this draconian – if we're going to sack every actor who doesn't look wholly racially pure, then we're going to have rather a lot of gaps, a lot of gaps, no question, this is going to affect a lot of people.

KIRSCH: Hubert, one or the other! When the party says that's how it is, then that's how it is! That's how we've got tae proceed! Nae ifs or buts! Ah mean, they could aw choose another job, one where they're nae so much in the public eye, ye ken? In an office or a factory or sumhin. Ah'm no saying that Polacek has tae leave the country or be sent tae a concentration camp, not at aw! But he's intolerable on stage! Unfortunately! If ah'm gooin' tae act in this theatre, then ah want us tae be an example for the whole German Reich! The first truly racially pure Aryan theatre! Unsullied! Immaculate! [Hubert, one or the other! When the party says that's how it is, then that's how it is! That's how we've got to proceed! No ifs or buts! I mean, they could all choose another job, one where they're not so much in the public eye, you know? In an office or a factory or something. I'm not saying that Polacek has to leave the country or be sent to a concentration camp, not at all! But he's intolerable on stage! Unfortunately! If I'm going to act in this theater, then I want us to be an example for the whole German Reich! The first truly racially pure Aryan theater! Unsullied! Immaculate!]

MEISEL: Yes, well, what shall I, I'm rather impressed, what you've just said, Herr Höllrigl, that's, yes, a good idea, a new idea, but a good idea. Herr Polacek, you are dismissed on the grounds of your un-Aryan appearance, which could endanger the standing of our theater.

Polacek looks helplessly at Strassky, then at Morovitz, then at Kirsch and then exits looking like a beaten dog.

STRASSKY: I never trusted him anyway. (*Catches sight of Olga.*) Well, Olga, I'm afraid you're next. (*To Kirsch:*) She hasn't got full proof of Aryan identity.

KIRSCH: Aye, ah realise that. [Yes, I realize that.]

MEISEL: Please, not until after the premiere, if that's all right with you? Replacing Walter Fürst is not a problem, but where am I going to get another Berta this late in the day?

KIRSCH: Verra well, but this disnae set a precedent. Ye'd better start looking for a replacement. [Very well, but this doesn't set a precedent. You'd better start looking for a replacement.]

MEISEL: Will do. (*Looks at his watch.*) Take a break, ladies and gentlemen. The auditors await me. (*Goes to the back, turns round.*) We meet here in thirty minutes, but punctually, please! (*Turns away, says whilst exiting:*) Another missed rehearsal, all this talk and no rehearsing, and don't the performances show it, *plus ça change.*

Helene exits, glancing back at Morovitz, who behaves as if he hasn't seen her, she goes sadly off. Olga also exits with tears in her eyes, Morovitz watches her go. The prompter also exits.

STRASSKY: (*in the meantime, to Kirsch*) Are you coming to the canteen?

KIRSCH: Naw, ah have to prepare maself for ma role. Tell's a tough part. [No, I have to prepare myself for my role. Tell's a tough part.]

STRASSKY: (*who has become rather wary of Kirsch*) Okay, see you later then.

Strassky goes off, Morovitz sets off after Olga.

KIRSCH: Gernot.

MOROVITZ: Yes, what is it?

KIRSCH: Come here a wee minute. [Come here a minute.]

Morovitz comes obediently over to Kirsch.

KIRSCH: (*sits down on a chair*) Ah jest happened tae witness that exchange between you and Frau Schwaiger... [I just happened to witness that exchange between you and Frau Schwaiger...]

MOROVITZ: I'm finishing with her anyway.

KIRSCH: Ah didnae say ye should finish wi' her, ah'm no a prig. Ah jest think she's a bit too much of a handful fur ye. [I didn't say you should finish with her, I'm not a prig. I just think she's a bit too much of a handful for you.]

MOROVITZ: You can say that again. She's exhausting me! Talk about highly strung!

KIRSCH: How long has this been gooin' on? [How long has this been going on?]

MOROVITZ: Two years.

KIRSCH: Aw aye? Two years? Is she married? [Oh yes? Two

years? Is she married?]

MOROVITZ: She was. To a Jew. He used to act in this theater.

KIRSCH: So, a Jew... That's no exactly in her favor, is it? [So, a Jew... That's not exactly in her favor, is it?]

MOROVITZ: She got divorced immediately, of course.

KIRSCH: And where is he noo? [And where is he now?]

MOROVITZ: In Switzerland. With the kids.

KIRSCH: Then ye two were havin' an affair when the Jew wiz still here? [Then you two were having an affair when the Jew was still here?]

MOROVITZ: Yes, we must have been, yes, definitely.

KIRSCH: An unfaithful wife. Ah dinnae like that. [An unfaithful wife. I don't like that.]

MOROVITZ: My God, Helene simply wasn't made for marriage. Heaven knows why she got married in the first place. And to him, of all people! He was a complete nohoper, a real loser. And he was blindly devoted to her, put up with everything. That's probably why it worked so well. It was enough for him just to be at her side. Although – he probably didn't see her much anyway in the final years. He pretty much brought up the children. By himself. He was a harmless sort of person. I didn't have anything against him. No one had anything against him. If he hadn't been a Jew, he'd still be standing here on this stage saying, "Sire, the horses are saddled."

KIRSCH: No a guid actor, then? [Not a good actor, then?]

MOROVITZ: Average, I'd say. With one exception. To celebrate the twenty-fifth anniversary of his becoming an actor he was allowed to play Shylock. And that really was impressive, somehow. I think he was acting out what he'd really always wanted to be: someone strong. But we put a spoke in his wheel. I'm almost sorry, in a way. (*Starts.*) Sorry!

KIRSCH: Nae pity for Jews, Gernot. [No pity for Jews, Gernot.]

MOROVITZ: Yes, I know, but you should have seen him. You're a theater fanatic, you would have understood.

KIRSCH: Tell me, d'ye like this Schwaiger wumin? Ah mean really? [Tell me, do you like this Schwaiger woman? I mean really?]

MOROVITZ: I was fascinated by her. And she IS very beautiful. I was utterly besotted. Completely and utterly. But now I can't stand to be with her.

KIRSCH: Now yer in love wi' Olga. [Now you're in love with Olga.]

Morovitz is startled.

KIRSCH: Are ye no? [Aren't you?]

Kirsch stares steadily at Morovitz, who nods.
KIRSCH: But Olga's got tae goo. [But Olga's got to go.]

MOROVITZ: (*after a while*) Than I'll go too. (*To Kirsch:*) Now you're disappointed in me, aren't you?

Kirsch doesn't answer.

MOROVITZ: I'm a National Socialist through and through, honestly, Herr Höllrigl. It doesn't matter about Polacek, he was basically an opportunist, and anyway, he's just a ham, but Olga's different, she really is a wonderful actress, she's going to be really big one day.

KIRSCH: That's no the reason why ye like her, is it? [That isn't the reason why you like her, is it?]

MOROVITZ: Partly, yes. I could never be with an untalented actress, I simply couldn't.

KIRSCH: That's much to yer credit. [That's much to your credit.]

MOROVITZ: But she's a wonderful person, too. She's someone I could marry, really. Stupid Aryan pass. Oh, I'm sorry!

KIRSCH: Verra well, tell her she's goat another three months. Ah'll see tae it. [Very well, tell her she's got another three months. I'll see to it.]

MOROVITZ (*shakes Kirsch's hand*) Thank you, Herr Höllrigl, thank you! I'll go and tell her straight away!

KIRSCH: Ye do that! [You do that!]

Morovitz exits, Meisel peers around the corner, having waited until Morovitz leaves. He now enters in a state of nervous excitement and walks up and down in front of Kirsch, who watches him calmly.

MEISEL: (*after a while, quite suddenly*) What shall I say? What shall I say? Words fail me, yes, quite simply. Speechless.

KIRSCH: When did you realize?

MEISEL: Just now! When you were talking about Rosenberg! Scales fell from my, although even at your audition I did sometimes think, this can't be, this can't really be, you did get a bit carried away there, eh, Kirsch, but on the other hand I thought maybe there really are people like that, maybe that's what they're like, I don't know enough about mountain dwellers and rural types since I never leave the city, hardly even the theater, you seem to have learned a bit from country farces, Kirsch, but at all events I'm, but first let me humbly, really most humbly apologize that I failed to recognize your talent for so long, phenomenal, truly phenomenal, and then, I wasn't actually there, when our tinpot Nazis decided to humiliate you on my stage, I regret that, I'm truly sorry –

KIRSCH: Would you have stood up to them if you had been there?

MEISEL: No, no, certainly not, because I've promised myself I'm going to outlive them, they're not going to destroy me, they'll have to, they're not taking over my theater, they're not ruining that, but, Herr Kirsch, I would have walked out, I wouldn't have stayed to witness it, absolutely not.

KIRSCH: Very courageous of you.

MEISEL: Are you going to take them out one after the other, is that what you intend?

KIRSCH: Maybe, amongst other things. We'll see.

MEISEL: Revenge, then, revenge. I understand, I can sympathize with that, yes, I can.

KIRSCH: Who says I won't take you out as well, Herr Meisel?

MEISEL: (*stares at him*) I hadn't thought of, yes, well, of course you'd be justified, I wasn't exactly, but, you know, when it comes to my theater, to saving my theater, I'm completely ruthless, nothing else matters.

KIRSCH: You did help me with Polacek beforehand.

MEISEL: Oh, you noticed, did you?

KIRSCH: I noticed.

MEISEL: But why Polacek, he's relatively harmless? Strassky now, I'd rather you got him off my back, he's genuinely dangerous, and a nuisance, a real nuisance.

KIRSCH: Patience, Herr Meisel. All in good time. With Polacek the opportunity just presented itself.

MEISEL: And as for Morovitz, he's not at all, he's just naive, not remotely malicious –

KIRSCH: (*gets up angrily*) All right, all right, what am I supposed to do, embrace him? Our young heartthrob?

MEISEL: Oh, you've noticed, well, but, one shouldn't forget that she was the one who, it wasn't him who, I mean, ahem, it's none of my business, forgive me.

KIRSCH: She didn't recognize me. (*Disappointed and despairing:*) She didn't recognize me! (*Laughs bitterly.*)

MEISEL: Your wife hasn't got eyes for anyone but herself, you ought to know that by – (*stops; then:*) If they find out about this, Kirsch, we'll all end up in a concentration camp, no question about it!

KIRSCH: You won't, Herr Meisel! If I managed to deceive everyone else, than why not you as well?

MEISEL: They'll be looking for a scapegoat. And who'll be the scapegoat? The theater manager! Please, Kirsch, do me one favor, one last act of revenge: Strassky! Revenge yourself on Strassky, destroy him, but then, I beg you, give it up, go away, disappear!

KIRSCH: No. This part I'm going to play to the end.

MEISEL: Is that your last word, Kirsch?

KIRSCH: My last word.

MEISEL: It's a lions' den! You've turned my theater into a lions' den! They'll tear you to pieces, Kirsch, to pieces! And don't expect God to send an angel to shut the lions' mouths either, you're not exactly Daniel, you know.

Kirsch smiles and makes a gesture of resignation.

MEISEL: Very well, in that case I'm compelled to, I shall be your comrade-in-arms, what choice do I…, what else can I do?

KIRSCH: Good. I could do with some support. By the way,

Herr Meisel, I feel obliged to tell you one thing: they WILL find out about this business. Through me. I intend to unmask myself.

MEISEL: (*appalled*) No!

KIRSCH: Of course I shall. What did you expect? That's the whole point. Do you really think vengeance is all I care about? Revenging myself on one or two insignificant individuals? I'll do that as well, of course, I admit to being that petty, but it can't be everything, it isn't enough. This is a matter of principle, Herr Meisel. I'm going to show up the whole system. So I have to tear off my mask. I have to show that behind the Tyrolean Aryan was the Jew, Arthur Kirsch. But not in the safety of Switzerland. Here, but here upon this bank and shoal of time. On this stage.

MEISEL: Then you're, you're, dead, dead!

Kirsch lifts his hands in a gesture of resignation.

MEISEL: Aren't you afraid?

KIRSCH: Of course I am. All the time.

He draws a pistol and shows it to Meisel, who stares at it in horror.

MEISEL: I see. So that's it? A suicide mission. How dreadful. You're a terrible man.

KIRSCH: No, not a suicide mission. I did contemplate suicide after I was driven out, up there in the mountains, in the night and the fog and the rain. It was only the thought of the children that held me back. No. Since I've embarked on this, I feel alive again, I've come alive. I was dead before.

Back then.

MEISEL: What's this for then? This murderous weapon?

KIRSCH: It's really only for emergencies, Herr Meisel. I won't be humiliated again. Never again. I don't intend to use this on myself. (*Puts the pistol away.*)

MEISEL: (*astonished*) I never would have guessed, I never would have guessed that you, even in my dreams, that you had this inside you – It's MY fault, all my fault, if I'd recognized what you really are, you would have been playing leading roles for the last twenty-five years, you would have had plenty of career satisfaction and would have gone into exile without a murmur, that's how I see it, I could box my own ears!

KIRSCH: Yes, and I'd be playing German SS officers in Hollywood films.

MEISEL: I give in, at all events I shall transfer my savings abroad. And what do you plan to do next, Herr Kirsch?

KIRSCH: (*smiling*) I shall play William Tell.

Blackout. Curtain.

SCENE 5

The premiere of William Tell. *Tremendous applause. The curtain rises to reveal the set for the last scene ("Valley in front of Tell's house, with the peaks that surround it"), the actors acknowledge – for the umpteenth time – the applause. These are: Kirsch as Tell, Helene as his wife Hedwig, Morovitz as Rudenz, Strassky as Gessler, Olga as Berta, also a few other main characters (played by extras), for instance, Werner,*

Stauffacher, Fürst, Melchtal, Baumgarten, Parricida, Gertrud and Tell's sons, Walter and William (and so on as needed). The applause reaches a crescendo at the entrance of the actors, we hear cries of "Bravo!" As instructed, the actors are supposed to respond not with a bow but with a Nazi salute, however, this is not wholly successful. Olga and four other actors remain faithful to the traditional bow, others do both, bowing with outstretched right arms. Only Kirsch, Helene, Strassky and Morovitz salute perfectly. Morovitz looks at Olga (who is standing quite far away from him) and waggles his outstretched arm to indicate that she, too, should salute, but she ignores him. Kirsch looks into the wings and signals to someone to enter, but they do not appear. Kirsch whispers to Morovitz (who is standing next to him) to go and fetch the missing person, Morovitz disappears and eventually drags the reluctant Meisel onto the stage. The applause becomes louder again, cries of "Bravo!" Meisel acknowledges this with a nervous gesture, a mixture of bow, sloppy Nazi salute and ordinary salute. The curtain falls, the applause continues, the curtain rises to reveal Kirsch and Helene side by side, they give a Nazi salute. Helene is thrilled, she squeezes Kirsch's arm tightly, then hugs him, the applause reaches a new crescendo. The curtain falls, the applause continues, the curtain rises again, Kirsch is alone on stage. At first he stands motionless with his hand raised, like a statue, then abruptly signals for the applause to end. Silence in the auditorium.

KIRSCH: Ladies and gentlemen, I –

Kirsch falls silent, astonished because the curtain has suddenly fallen. He immediately comes out in front of the curtain, Meisel catches his arm and tries to hold him back and is almost dragged out by Kirsch. He looks at him imploringly, then vanishes.

KIRSCH: Ladies and gentlemen, at last ah can speak in ma own tongue again! Lads and lassies, ma fellow theater-lovers, ah'm so happy ah can hardly speak, but let me heave ma heart into ma mooth! I cannae let ye go hame wi'oot tellin' ye that this is the happiest day of ma whole life! (*Turns away overcome with emotion and wipes his eyes.*) Forgive me, ah dinnae usually weep, the last time wiz when ah buried ma wife, naw, it wiz when ma three best cows got struck by lightning, but I cannae help it, ma eyes jest startit watering. That ah'm standing here today, that ah'm playing William Tell, the greatest German character of aw the German classics, by our great German playwright, Friedrich Schiller, and that ye aw accept me, me a simple farmer, that ye like ma acting, I cannae believe it, it's like a dream, a bonny unreal dream. Thank ye, all of ye. Come again. Guid night, and Heil Hitler! [Ladies and gentlemen, at last I can speak in my own tongue again! My fellow theater-lovers, I'm so happy I can hardly speak, but let me heave my heart into my mouth! I can't let you go home without telling you that this is the happiest day of my whole life! (*Turns away overcome with emotion and wipes his eyes.*) Forgive me, I don't usually weep, the last time was when I buried my wife, no, it was when my three best cows got struck by lightning, but I can't help it, my eyes just started watering. That I'm standing here today, that I'm playing William Tell, the greatest German character of all the German classics, by our great German playwright, Friedrich Schiller, and that you all accept me, me a simple farmer, that you like my acting, I can't believe it, it's like a dream, a beautiful unreal dream. Thank you, all of you. Come again. Good night, and Heil Hitler!]

Stormy applause and cheers, Kirsch disappears behind the curtain, the applause dies down, lights up in the auditorium, lights down again, the curtain rises again. Working lights on stage. From backstage right comes the sound of an Alpenhorn being blown, then applause, then sounds of a crowd of people enjoying themselves. The first-night party is taking place in an implied room somewhere backstage. Eder and his stage crew enter from up left.

EDER: Okay, take it all down. Let's get this stuff off.

The stage crew make a start. Meisel comes on from the direction of the party.

MEISEL: (*doped up on tranquillizers and so speaks more slowly, but naturally in the same idiosyncratic style*) Leave it, leave it, Eder, we're extending the run, the demand for tickets, incredible, I had no faith in this enterprise, but after this phenomenal, wasn't the applause fantastic, Eder, fantastic, I've never known, nothing like this.

EDER: Old Höllrigl's really good, too.

MEISEL: Isn't he, I'm pleased you think so, Eder, I know no one pulls the wool over your eyes, you know good acting when you see it, please, gentlemen, leave everything as it is, come and celebrate with the rest of us, go and join in the party, there's a buffet with genuine Swiss cheese, quite superb, donated by the Swiss Milk Marketing Board, and there's a band of Alpenhorn players.

EDER: Cheers, Herr Meisel, I like a bit of Swiss cheese.

He waves his crew over and they all head backstage. Kirsch comes towards them (no longer in his Tell costume).

EDER: Congratulations, Herr Höllrigl, a first class performance!

Kirsch nods his thanks, Eder and his crew go off, Meisel goes over to Kirsch.

MEISEL: Kirsch, you're going to kill me, I almost had a nervous breakdown, I thought now he's going to do it, he's going to unmask himself, it's all over, when you started ..., to the audience.

KIRSCH: No, the time isn't yet right, Herr Meisel.

MEISEL: (*squeezes Kirsch's hand with both hands*) Thank you! What a relief! Thank you! But might I ask you (*takes a pill*) to inform me beforehand when you're planning to reveal yourself, because I'll never survive this …, look at me, I'm a nervous wreck!

KIRSCH: I'm sorry, Herr Meisel, but I don't know myself. When the time is right…

MEISEL: You'll let me, beforehand, won't you?

KIRSCH: I can't promise anything, Herr Meisel. It will be a sudden impulse, I presume.

MEISEL: Martyrdom, then, martyrdom, you torturer, you wonderful torturer. The Nazis will never have a better Tell, actually I begrudge them that, they don't deserve –

Polacek enters, very down-at-heel, clutching a two-liter bottle of white wine.

MEISEL: Polacek! What are you doing here?

POLACEK: (*drunk*) I'm sorry, I'm sorry, I don't want to offend you with my Jew face. (*Boxes his own ears.*) I've come to do homage to the great master! Saw the performance, from the gallery (*points upwards, then starts to weep loudly*), it was incredible, incredible, Herr Höllrigl, Herr Höllrigl, let me kiss your feet!

He falls weeping to his knees, Kirsch comes over and helps him up.

KIRSCH: Come now, Herr Polacek, there's no need for that. (*Starts, because he has just spoken without an accent.*) Gi' it a rest, ah cannae stand boot-lickers! [Give it a rest, I can't stand boot-lickers!]

MEISEL: Polacek, this is really, go home at once and sleep off this, what kind of behavior is this?!

POLACEK: I'm doing homage to the great master! (*Kneels in front of Kirsch again.*) My master, the great master!

KIRSCH: (*pulling him up*) Polacek, pull yerself taegether! (*Shakes him.*) Understand? [Polacek, pull yourself together! (*Shakes him.*) Understand?]

POLACEK: Don't look at my Jew face, not my Jew face! (*Staggers off.*) I'm not worthy! I'm not worthy! I'm not worthy!

MEISEL: Well, he's got a bad case of, really, he belongs in a, but come along, Kirsch, let's rejoin the happy throng, come and bathe in your glory.

KIRSCH: I've bathed enough, thank you, it's all getting a bit too much for me.

MEISEL: What, already? But Kirsch, it's only just started, this is only the beginning, you said so your –, this is what you wanted, isn't it?

KIRSCH: Yes, it's what I wanted. But I underestimated it. I'm not really made for all this. All the reporters, all the photographers (*shakes his head*), I wish I was in my Alpine meadow, far away from all this.

MEISEL: Watch out, don't immerse yourself too deeply in

Benedikt Höllrigl or you'll suddenly find you've turned into the real thing.

KIRSCH: I wish! – Please, Herr Meisel, you go ahead, give them some excuse, I'd like to be alone, just for a few minutes.

MEISEL: Very well, but make sure you come along soon, all right, you Teutonic hero, you!

Kirsch nods, Meisel goes off upstage, Kirsch sits down somewhere on the set, he is weary. He suddenly feels a pain in his heart and puts his hand on his chest. After a while Olga comes on from backstage (also out of costume), looks at him and shakes her head laughing.

KIRSCH: Did ye want tae see me, Fräulein Sternberg? [Did you want to see me, Fräulein Sternberg?]

OLGA: I did, Herr Kirsch.

KIRSCH: Oh God, you've recognized me too?

OLGA: Yes, this evening, during the performance. All through rehearsals I kept thinking, why is this yokel hamming it up so much? This doesn't feel right, there's something fishy about this. And then today, at the premiere, you were suddenly completely real, completely believable as Tell.

KIRSCH: Yes, well, I've got to ham it up a bit, play the old horny-handed son of toil. You know how it is. I haven't got the dialect down quite pat, so I need a crutch, I have to overdo it slightly, like any actor.

OLGA: (*shakes her head laughing*) It's a crazy idea, absolutely crazy. I'd never have thought it of you, Herr Kirsch.

KIRSCH: Me neither.

OLGA: (*looks at him, sits down next to him, then*) I'm Jewish, Herr Kirsch.

Kirsch looks at her in surprise.

OLGA: I only pretended not to know who my father was. And now Gernot's just told me that Strassky's given orders to have me investigated. There's a special office for it, run by the Gestapo.

She suddenly starts to cry, tries to suppress it, but can't. Kirsch puts his arm around her to comfort her.

KIRSCH: Don't worry, Olga, I'll deal with them.

OLGA: How? How? They'll find out about me!

KIRSCH: I'll think of something. I've got pretty good at Shakespearean intrigue. You go back to the party.

OLGA: (*gets up, wipes her eyes*) Thank you, Herr Kirsch, thank you!

KIRSCH: No, thank YOU, Fräulein Olga. You were the only one who stood up for me. That's not something I'll forget.

Olga goes off, Kirsch wonders how he could help her. Helene comes on carrying two glasses of champagne. Once again, she is stunningly dressed.

HELENE: But of course! Where else would our divine Tell be but on stage? Our fiery prophet! Well, wasn't that a triumph?

Kirsch gets up, Helene gives him a glass, then clinks hers against his.

HELENE: To you!

KIRSCH: Tae the both of us! [To both of us!]

They drink.

HELENE: Tomorrow your picture will be in every paper in the German Reich. (*She sees his weary expression.*) You aren't pleased? You aren't rejoicing? – You're homesick, aren't you?

Kirsch nods.

HELENE: I have some news for you that will banish your homesickness entirely.

Kirsch looks at her.

HELENE: (*delightedly*) The Minister is coming! Dr. Goebbels!

KIRSCH: Naw! [No!]

HELENE: He is! I've just spoken with him on the telephone. He's coming to one of the next performances!

KIRSCH: Ye cannae be serious! [You're joking!]

HELENE: Of course I am! I told him about you weeks ago, when we were shooting in Berlin. He was most intrigued. And now that I've told him what a huge triumph it is, he's going to come and see it!

KIRSCH: Well, cheers!

HELENE: I'm going to make you a prophecy, Herr Höllrigl.

It won't be long before we're both standing before the film cameras.

KIRSCH: Ah dinnae deserve this. [I don't deserve this.]

HELENE: Of course you deserve it! So be happy! What's the matter?

KIRSCH: It's no jest homesickness, Frau Schwaiger, it's another kind of sickness too. [It's not just homesickness, Frau Schwaiger, it's another kind of sickness too.]

HELENE: What kind?

Kirsch is silent.

HELENE: Come on, you can tell me! Out with it! Perhaps I can help.

KIRSCH: Ah've got whit they call feelings. [I've got what they call feelings.]

HELENE: Feelings?

Kirsch nods.

HELENE: What kind of feelings?

KIRSCH: Love. Love... Funny, when ah say that, ah dinnae believe it maself. Where ah come frae, in the mountains, ye ken, we dinnae use the word "love." We jest dinnae say it. Ah mean, we ken fine whit love is, o' course, or falling in love. Or when yer keen on someone. But we dinnae use the word "love." And ah ask maself, could it be that this so-called love isnae really real? That it's jest play-acting? Sumhin our betters read aboot in books? Is it a game that us simple folk dinnae play? Where ah come frae we say: ah like ye, ah need ye, ah want ye. Sometimes even: ah've got tae have ye. And verra often: yer mine. But it won't be any different wi' ye lot. It's jest that ye use the word love for aw that. [Love. Love... Funny, when I say that, I don't believe it myself. Where I come from, in the mountains, we don't use the word love. We just don't say it. I mean, we know what love is, of course, or falling in love. Or when you're keen on someone. But we don't use the word "love." And I ask myself, could it be that this so-called love isn't really real? That it's just playacting? Something our betters read about in books? Is it a game that we simple folk don't play? Where I come from we say: I like you, I need you, I want you. Sometimes even: I've got to have you. And very often: you're mine. But it won't be any different with your lot. It's just that you use the word love for all that.]

HELENE: How can you say that, Herr Höllrigl? Do you think you can lecture me about love? Just imagine! Perhaps there's more to you than meets the eye! Why, you're a philosopher! A peasant philosopher! – But come now, tell me what you really mean, I don't understand.

KIRSCH: (*moves a step or two away from her, then turns round*) Ah love ye, Frau Schwaiger. [I love you, Frau Schwaiger.]

Helene stares at him in astonishment, he turns away from her.

KIRSCH: Ah'm sorry, ah cannae help masel'. And ah ken fine that it's impossible. That's why ah'm sad. That's why I cannae join in the celebrations. If ye could only see whit ah really am, that'd be enough, then ah'd be happy. [I'm sorry, I can't help myself. And I know that it's impossible. That's why I'm sad. That's why I can't join in the celebrations. If you could only see what I really am, that'd be enough, then I'd be happy.]

HELENE: (*stares at him, then*) Dear Herr Höllrigl, please don't fall in love with me. I'm nothing special. It's all just illusion. Show. Theater.

KIRSCH: (*turns round to face her*) Och aye, ye are something special. Sich a bonny wumin, sich a talented wumin. And ye have a soul, a right bonny one. If ye look closely enough. [Oh yes, you are something special. Such a beautiful woman, such a talented woman. And you have a soul, a beautiful one. If you look closely enough.]

HELENE: (*moved*) I fear that my soul spends all its time looking in the mirror. Don't love me, Herr Höllrigl, you'll only get hurt. There was a man who loved me, once, he was rather like you. Less lively than you, less flamboyant, but his nature was essentially very similar to yours.

KIRSCH: Aye – and? [Yes – and?]

HELENE: I made him very unhappy. I was unfaithful to him. You see, Herr Höllrigl, I can't be faithful, I'm simply incapable. (*Gives a despairing laugh.*) I need mirrors, mirrors, mirrors!

KIRSCH: He's deid, is he, yer husband? [He's dead, is he, your husband?]

HELENE: No. I left him. Abandoned him. When he most needed me. Please don't ask me any more, Herr Höllrigl.

Kirsch gazes at her for a long time. She gets irritated, he goes up to her and stands very close in front of her.

KIRSCH: I love you, Helene.

She looks into his eyes, suddenly recognizes him and faints, he catches her, carries her over to a chair, sits down with her on his lap and strokes her hair and face. She comes to herself, looks at him, staggers up with a shriek and stares at him.

HELENE: Arthur?

KIRSCH: Yes, Leni.

She cannot believe it. Kirsch gets up slowly, suddenly she flings herself at him with a shriek and pummels him. He lets her, she gives up and embraces him, sobbing.

HELENE: You horrible, horrible man! Why are you doing this? Why are you doing this to me?

KIRSCH: Don't ask me, I don't know myself anymore. It all suddenly seems so childish, so absurd. – But I do know one thing, Leni, I love you, I always have done. In spite of everything. And another thing: I always knew, and I was always jealous. I'm jealous now.

Helene sobs, looks at him, kisses him, then runs off weeping loudly (not in the direction of the party). Kirsch watches her go, sits down again, broods for a while, then suddenly has an idea, looks in the direction of the party and goes off that way. Eder and the stage crew come on. Eder is holding an enormous piece of Swiss cheese, his crew have smaller pieces. Each of them has an open bottle of beer.

EDER: Now that's what I call cheese! I reckon I'll move to Zurich after all, they've got a good theater there. Then I wouldn't have to put up with this Nazi cheese.

He goes off left with the others. Olga and Strassky (in SA uniform) enter from the party, Strassky is holding a wine glass.

STRASSKY: Olga, there's no point in trying to dissuade me! The procedure's been set in motion now, and anyway, I take a firm line on this sort of thing.

Olga looks at him imploringly.

STRASSKY: What about Höllrigl? Do you think I could get him to agree? He'd tear me to pieces! The man's an absolute fanatic!

OLGA: We were always good friends, Hubert.

STRASSKY: Not anymore, Fräulein Sternberg.

OLGA: I love you, Hubert.

STRASSKY: (*hesitates, then*) Oh really, stop it, what's that supposed to mean?

OLGA: No, really, I love you.

STRASSKY: Oh please, don't try to get round me this way! Do you think I'm stupid?

She looks at him "lovingly."

STRASSKY: You're Morovitz's girlfriend!

OLGA: No, I'm not. He's wants me to be, but I only want you.

STRASSKY: And why is that?

OLGA: You're a man. You're everything a man should be. A real man.

STRASSKY: Really?

OLGA: Yes. And I have to confess something. When you yelled at me that time, over that business with Kirsch, it made my spine tingle.

STRASSKY: Really?

OLGA: Yes.

STRASSKY: The other women always cringe when I shout at them, it makes me want to – it gets on my nerves.

OLGA: I cringed too. No wonder. Your voice is a powerful organ, Hubert. But it was a wonderful feeling, your voice went right through me, right to the marrow.

STRASSKY: Really?

OLGA: I dream about you. That you're shouting at me, humiliating me. That you're grabbing hold of me, seizing me.

They stare at each other. Olga takes a step towards Strassky, suddenly he pulls her brutally to him and tries to kiss her, she pushes him away.

OLGA: No! You've got to shout at me first. Shout at me. Please!

STRASSKY: (*looks around to make sure no one is watching*) But I'm telling you now, if there's anything wrong with you, with your racial background, then I want nothing to do with you, I'll drop you like a ton of bricks.

OLGA: Drop me, have nothing to do with me, just let me be with a real man for once, that's all I ask of you.

STRASSKY: (*looks around again*) You slut! You bitch!

OLGA: (*flinches*) Yes! Yes! More! More! (*She keeps this up whilst he abuses her, spurring him on.*)

Eder appears upstage and watches in amazement.

STRASSKY: I'm going to kill you, you slut! I'll tear your head off! I'll slit you open! I'll cut you to pieces, you stupid bitch, you cow, you moron! Stop gaping like that or I'll smash your face in! You Jewish slut!

OLGA: (*suddenly severe and matter-of-fact*) Not that, Hubert, I don't like it. Until anyone can prove the opposite I'm a good German girl, all right?

STRASSKY: Sorry.

OLGA: Now I'm not in the mood anymore.

STRASSKY: Sorry. (*Thinks for a moment, then shouts:*) You Aryan slut, you German whore, you!

OLGA: Yes! Yes! More! More!
Kirsch, Meisel, Morovitz and the two Gestapo officers come on. Kirsch looks at the officers and puts his finger to his lips.

STRASSKY: Come here, you, I'm going to wring your neck! (He *pulls her savagely to him and kisses her.*) Shall I smash your head against the wall, shall I? Shall I smash your head against the wall?

OLGA: Do what you want! (*Kisses him.*) Smash me against the wall, tear me limb from limb, tie me up, whip me, do what you want!

They kiss. Strassky has completely lost control, seizes her by the arm, starts to drag her into "Tell's cottage," then suddenly notices his audience and freezes. Olga calmly takes his hand, which is still gripping her arm, undoes his fingers and steps away from him. Morovitz stares at the two in deep disappointment and then runs off.

KIRSCH: So that's how it is. Comrade Strassky. Contaminating the German bluid. Engaging in sexual relations wi' a woman of inferior race. And ah thought weel of ye! (*Spits contemptuously.*) [So that's how it is. Comrade Strassky. Contaminating the German blood. Engaging in sexual relations with a woman of inferior race. And I thought well of you!]

STRASSKY: (*stammering*) But, but that hasn't been, who says that she's Jewish, her mother's an, it's only her father's papers –

KIRSCH: (*yells at him*) Shall AH smash YER heid against the wall, hey?! Ye lily-livered fraud! Ye ken damn well she's a Jew! [Shall I smash YOUR head against the wall, hey?! You lily-livered fraud! You know damn well she's a Jew!]

Strassky, shrinking in horror, looks at Olga for help.

OLGA: Oh, it's like that now, is it?

FIRST GESTAPO OFFICER: Herr Strassky, Fräulein

Sternberg, you're under arrest.

KIRSCH: (*to the Gestapo Officers, beckoning them over*) A wee word.

Kirsch takes the First Gestapo Officer's arm and goes downstage with him, the Second Gestapo Officer follows, Kirsch beckons Meisel over as well. They then speak quietly enough that Olga and Strassky can't quite hear what they're saying, although they listen anxiously.

KIRSCH: Ye'd be doin' us a big favour, the theatre ah mean, if ye'd leave the Sternberg wumin wi' us for a day or two. [You'd be doing us a big favor, the theater I mean, if you'd leave the Sternberg woman with us for a day or two.]

FIRST GESTAPO OFFICER: But Herr Höllrigl, with all due respect –

KIRSCH: Jest a day or two. We've nae understudy for her. Ah wantit to have her thrown oot the minute ah found out about her – did I no, Herr Meisel? [Just a day or two. We've no understudy for her. I wanted to have her thrown out the minute I found out about her – didn't I, Herr Meisel?]

MEISEL: That's right, absolutely, I tried to find a substitute straight away, but unfortunately, so far. If you deprive me of Fräulein Sternberg I shall regretfully be compelled to cancel the next few performances.

FIRST GESTAPO OFFICER: Heaven forbid!

MEISEL: It would be a catastrophe, a catastrophe, this is the biggest success this theater has ever, I've never heard such cheering, never.

FIRST GESTAPO OFFICER: (*nods*) We cheered as well, didn't we?

The Second Gestapo Officer nods.

KIRSCH: Ah'll keep an eye on her, make sure she disnae make a run for it. Besides, she loves the part, it's the best she's ever had. [I'll keep an eye on her, make sure she doesn't make a run for it. Besides, she loves the part, it's the best she's ever had.]

FIRST GESTAPO OFFICER: There's nothing Jewish about her acting, I'll give her that.

He looks at his colleague, who nods in agreement.

FIRST GESTAPO OFFICER: Very well then, just this once, since this is a historic occasion in a way, with you, Herr Höllrigl.

KIRSCH: That's grand. Heil Hitler! [That's great. Heil Hitler!]

FIRST GESTAPO OFFICER: Heil Hitler!

The First Gestapo Officer goes up to the astonished Strassky and takes him roughly by the arm, he exits with him, followed by the Second Gestapo Officer. Olga watches them go, unable to believe it. Meisel puts his hand on his heart, scarcely able to bear the tension, and then sinks into a chair. At the back of the stage Eder claps.

MEISEL: What a relief! What a relief! What a blessed day!

EDER: You can say that again. That's two down.

OLGA: And what about me?

KIRSCH: You'll be fine. We're keeping you, Olga.

She cannot believe it.

KIRSCH: For the moment. But don't worry, I'll sort it out.

Olga comes up and hugs him. Eder comes over.

EDER: One of yer best performances, Miss, honest! Congratulations!

Olga wipes her mouth with a little noise of disgust. Morovitz comes in, very worked up.

MOROVITZ: (*to Olga*) I never would have thought it of you, never! And with that swine...! Like that, in that way! And you a Jew! It's, it's perverted!

KIRSCH: Herr Morovitz, it was just –

MOROVITZ: (*almost in tears*) You slut! I hate you! (*Runs off.*)

OLGA: (*imploringly to Kirsch*) Can I tell him? Please!

Kirsch moves his head in a gesture of assent. Olga runs after Morovitz.

MEISEL: This is a madhouse, God in heaven, I can't stand it any– ! Theater here, life there! Theater here, life there, neatly separated! That's how it ought to be, full stop! Otherwise we'd go, it'll all, haywire, Kirsch, you're driving me insane!

KIRSCH: Sorry, Herr Meisel!

EDER: Things are getting a bit tight, Herr Kirsch. The make-up artist recognized you straight away, well, she would, wouldn't she, and I just heard in there (*points in the direction of the party*) that two of the actors have as well, Prüller and Haushofer. And my lads've known for ages, though I never told 'em nothing. None of them's a Nazi but even so, this'll spread like wildfire. I doubt if everyone'll keep their mouth shut.

KIRSCH: I'll soon be finished here.

EDER: I'll keep an eye out. They'll have to get past me first. And there's this secret passage I know about, it leads from under the stage into one of the houses opposite. One of the previous directors had it built because he lived over there and didn't like getting wet.

KIRSCH: Thank you, Herr Eder, that's worth knowing.

MEISEL: Thirty performances, Kirsch! At least do another thirty performances!

KIRSCH: (*looks at him; then*) I think I've got to get drunk. (*Goes off in the direction of the party*.)

MEISEL: Gently, Kirsch, gently, don't you dare, not too much, for God's sake, in moderation, I beg you, Kirsch, in moderation, otherwise – (*to Eder:*) what if he starts blabbing, then we're all, I'd better go after him. (*Hurries after Kirsch.*)

Lights down. After a while a new scene starts. It is morning, the stage is almost completely dark. Kirsch is lying asleep somewhere on stage. Polacek appears with his now empty wine bottle and wanders around, swaying unsteadily.

POLACEK (*drunk*) Blow winds and crack your cheeks! Rage,

blow!
You cataracts and hurricanoes, spout
Till you have drenched our steeples, drowned the cocks!
You sulphurous and thought-executing fires,
Vaunt couriers of oak-cleaving thunderbolts,
Singe my white head! And thou, all-shaking thunder,
Strike flat the thick rotundity o' the world,
Crack nature's moulds, all germens spill at once
That make ingrateful man!
(Comes to the front of the stage and speaks into the auditorium, quietly, as if he has suddenly sobered up.) Last night I had a curious dream. I saw and I heard an eagle, flying in mid-heaven, saying with a great voice woe, woe, woe, for them that dwell on the earth. And lo! there was a great earthquake, and the Sun became black as a sackcloth of hair, and the Moon became as blood; and the stars of heaven fell to the earth; and the heaven departed as a scroll when it is rolled up. And I heard a voice as of a trumpet crying forth Earth, give up your dead! And the naked fields began to labor and brought forth skulls and ribs and jaws and bones! *(He begins to scurry around whimpering – and now he really does seem like an elderly, despairing Jew – until he stumbles against a piece of scenery and falls to the ground, right next to the sleeping Kirsch. He sees him and stares).* The master. The great master. Tired. Having a little snooze. On the Day of Judgment.

Polacek crawls across to Kirsch, stares into his face, suddenly feels an powerful impulse to kill him, raises his wine bottle to strike a lethal blow, then realizes what he's doing, puts the bottle down and reaches out his hands to strangle Kirsch. As he nears his throat he pauses again, looks around, sees something, gets up, goes over and fetches Tell's crossbow, which is propped up against a piece of scenery, examines it carefully, cocks it, goes over to Kirsch, takes aim, then changes his mind again, looks around, sees a large rock, puts down the crossbow, goes over to the rock and picks it up, lifting it over his head, but, because the rock is made of cardboard and is very light, falls over backwards and lies there unconscious.

After a while the ordinary working lights go up. Meisel and Eder enter (dressed as on the previous evening, but with hats and coats over their clothes), Meisel is once again on the edge of a nervous breakdown. They start to search around.

MEISEL: This is a disaster, Eder, an utter disaster!

EDER: We'll find him, Herr Meisel, he can't have disappeared off of the face of the earth.

Kirsch awakes with a hangover and sits up. The other two don't notice him but he sees them.

MEISEL: He's shot himself, he's jumped off a bridge, he's been arrested, at the very least he's on the train to Tyrol, why is he doing this to me, Eder, why?

EDER: *(catching sight of Polacek)* There he is. *(Goes over, bends over the sleeping figure.)* No, it ain't him. It's Polacek.

Meisel sits down, exhausted, and swallows a couple of pills. Kirsch is sitting directly behind him.

MEISEL: I tell you, Eder, I'm going to retire, this is too, no, really.

Eder sees Kirsch and grins.

MEISEL: Stop grinning like an idiot, Eder, it gets on my – (*He turns around, sees Kirsch and stands up.*) Kirsch, under any other circumstances I would sack you on the spot! All night long, all night long we have been searching for, in every night club in the district, in your hotel, in the gutters, look at my shoes, handmade in Hungary, Kirsch, almost died of worry, and where are you, sleeping here on the, you and this sot, Polacek, this is a madhouse, my theater was always a haven of tranquility, of equanimity, of civilized behavior, and you're making a madhouse, Kirsch, how could you do this to, how could you?

KIRSCH: I'm sorry, Herr Meisel. I'm afraid I didn't follow your advice. (*Clutches his aching head.*) Oh God! I was easily as drunk as our esteemed colleague over there (*points at Polacek.*). I hope I didn't swear eternal friendship to him.

MEISEL: That's all I need, look Eder, dispose of Polacek, will you —

Helene (differently dressed from the previous evening) enters hurriedly, carrying a few newspapers.

HELENE: I've been looking for you everywhere! Look, Arthur, the reviews! (*She stops in horror, putting her hand to her mouth.*)

KIRSCH: They already know, Leni.

HELENE: Oh!

EDER: What do they say then, Frau Schwaiger?

HELENE: (*opens one of the reviews and reads aloud:*) "A Peasant Tell — Höllrigl bestrides the stage like a colossus. When he speaks, a hot mountain wind seems to blow from the stage, rising to a storm of fire fierce enough to burn away the old social order, razing it to the ground."

MEISEL: (*takes a newspaper out of her hand and reads aloud*) "Probably the most memorable premiere since the original first performance. Meisel's mastery of theatrical form reaches its zenith with this production." – Oh, thank you! – "The exquisitely painstaking and somewhat over-intellectual director and the earthy uneducated peasant – the combination could have been a disaster, but what a magnificent triumph it has turned out be!"

HELENE: (*reading from another newspaper*) "A Peasant Triumphs – this Tell stands firmly rooted in the soil of his homeland, unshakeable, the embodiment and symbol of the pure Aryan hero, prepared to feed the earth with his own blood that we might harvest a better future – no one will ever equal the achievement of this magnificent new discovery."

MEISEL: (*reads on*) "Your reviewer confesses that he came close to leaping out of his comfortable theater seat" – oh, thank you. – "seizing a weapon and joining Tell in his righteous struggle. How often in recent years have we had to watch diluted, soggy, liberal, sometimes even Marxist or thoroughly degenerate productions of our classical heritage, frequently performed by decadent Jewish actors, who could never be capable of arousing a German heart" – Thanks a lot, what have I done? This is dreadful! (*Throws the newspaper away.*)

HELENE: (*reads*) "There has never been a better Tell and we will never see a better Tell in all the years to come. Germany has lost a farmer and gained a great actor."

KIRSCH: That's enough!

Meisel takes another newspaper from Helene and examines the reviews.

HELENE: You should be pleased, Arthur! You've defeated

them!

KIRSCH: They can't be defeated. Not like this. I feel so empty. Like a child that's been given too many Christmas presents.

MEISEL: (*Hasn't been listening, looks up from his newspaper*) Sixty performances! At least sixty performances, Kirsch! I'll pay you double!

KIRSCH: What I need now is some sleep.

Kirsch goes off, slowly and wearily. The others watch him go.

HELENE: Arthur! (*Runs after him.*) YOU are a hero! YOU are a hero! Not these stupid little boys I'm always chasing after! I had such a great man at my side and never noticed it! Oh please, forgive me! Please forgive me! (*Embraces him, then starts in horror.*) Oh God, oh God, the minister! Dr. Goebbels! Oh God, I'm done for! What have you done to me? What have you done to me? You wouldn't do that to me, would you, Arthur?

Kirsch doesn't answer.

HELENE: Think of our children!

KIRSCH: I am thinking of our children, Leni.

HELENE: He won't put up with this! He'll kill us! He'll kill us when he finds out!

KIRSCH: Surely dear, charming Dr. Goebbels, who so loves to dine with you, wouldn't do that?

HELENE: That's not true, it's not true, Arthur! There is nothing between us, it's just a malicious rumor! I mean, I admit he admires me, and why shouldn't I…? It's flattering, Arthur, the Minister for Propaganda…, that sort of thing has a positive effect on one's earnings, you know, and I have to think about the children's future!

KIRSCH: That's good. That means we're both thinking about our children's future. (*Goes off upstage left, turns round again.*) Forgive me, Leni. Why should I be more jealous of your Dr. Goebbels than of all the others? (*Exits.*)

HELENE: This will kill me!

MEISEL: (*dryly*) This will kill all of us. We'll be the first theatrical ensemble in Auschwitz.

Helene gives a loud sob, then runs off.

MEISEL: (*to Eder*) You'd better show me this tunnel, all right?

EDER: Be a pleasure, Herr Meisel.

MEISEL: (*exiting right*) You can come with me to Zurich if you like, Eder.

EDER: Zurich, any time, Herr Meisel. Where there's Swiss cheese, there's hope, that's what I say. (*Goes over to Polacek and prods him with his foot.*) Hey! Herr Polacek! Hey! (*Shakes him.*)

POLACEK: (*Wakes up and looks at him in confusion*) Herr Eder, I am determined to prove a villain.

EDER: I'm sure you are, Herr Polacek. You can find your

own way out, can't you? (*Exits upstage.*)

Polacek gets up onto his knees, stares into the audience, stands up unsteadily, comes further downstage, almost falls into the auditorium and stares at the audience.

POLACEK: I, that am curtail'd of this fair proportion,
Cheated of feature by dissembling Nature,
Deform'd, unfinished, sent before my time
Into this breathing world scarce half made up –
And that so lamely and unfashionable
That dogs bark at me as I halt by them!
I am determined to prove a villain!

He staggers off. Curtain.

SCENE 6

The curtain rises. Set for William Tell. *Goebbels is standing at a lectern in an elegant, double-breasted suit. To his right and left are two SS adjutants in ceremonial uniform (one has a box with a medal in it). Behind them the actors from* William Tell *are lined up in costume and make-up: Kirsch as Tell, Helene as his wife Hedwig, Morovitz as Rudenz, an extra as Gessler, Olga as Berta, Meisel and any others mentioned in Scene 5. Helene is close to fainting for sheer excitement, Meisel has stuffed himself with tranquillizers, he is stoical but deathly white. Kirsch's heart is giving him trouble, he can't helping feeling for it with his left hand.*

GOEBBELS: National Socialism loves the theater. Not everyone has always been aware of this. Some people are unaware of it to this day. For we National Socialists used to hate the theater. We despised it. We only entered it to cry out our revulsion onto the abused stage! What the theater had been turned into by the writers, the directors and the actors, this heap of dregs and garbage, this chaotic lunatic asylum, this dreary laboratory of helpless experimenters, this had been crying out to heaven for decades! For someone like me, who for years fought in vain against the prostitution of the German stage to cultural bolshevism and moral decline, to the elevation of perverts and criminals, to a so-called modernism that was out of touch with the modern age, for someone like me this evening is a grand affirmation of everything we have stood for, a cause for celebration! The theater has become the place where the German nation lives out her destiny, her rise and fall, her transformation, her sacrifices, and the purification of her spirit. The Germanic hero, his victory or his tragic defeat, is the noblest subject of a dramatic art that is truly German. Tragedy must be harsh and merciless. As in the drama of classical antiquity, man must be true to his destiny. What we demand, comrades, is action! Action! We demand action in politics and we demand action in art! We require men of action and not egg-heads! We, the racially aware, no longer care what the degenerate Prince of Denmark does NOT do, we care which deeds the virile Fortinbras performs for the state! We, the racially aware, demand a new kind of actor. You have seen its pattern here on this stage. Alert, skilful manliness (*indicates Morovitz*), harsh, austere beauty (*indicates Olga*), the loving, self-sacrificing mother (*indicates Helene*), the father, the leader, the warrior, the heroic man, the very image of the German oak (*indicates Kirsch*)! Of all the arts, comrades, the theater must intervene most decisively in the racial question. For it is the most intimately concerned with blood and with bodies. It is THE artistic activity in which corporeality, the racial soul and racial values are made manifest. And, comrades, that is why the theater must be wholly purified of alien blood. Imagine Faust played by a Jew, Gretchen played by a Jewess! Impossible! Faustian striving will always be a book with seven seals to the Jewish understanding, because it is so wholly alien to their nature. Imagine William Tell, this embodiment of the German national character, played by a Jew! Impossible! Race and worldview, race and mental processes are so powerfully and so inextricably intertwined that even the shrewdest attempt at assimilation and understanding cannot succeed in simulating them. My fellow countrymen, since the turn of the century we had a manifestly Jewish German theater and we have destroyed that completely! And what did the foreign press vindictively predict? That Germany would become culturally impoverished, Germany would sink into a mindless banality without the Jews! Nonsense, and brilliantly disproved! And this evening, fellow countrymen, is the greatest cultural-political triumph the German Reich could ever celebrate! The theater has become once again the citadel of the German spirit! Germany is once again the motherland of world theater! I thank you all in the name of the Führer, and my thanks go especially to you, my esteemed comrade, Benedikt Höllrigl, because we owe this triumph primarily to you. It is my privilege to award you this medal, on behalf of the Führer.

Stormy applause, reporters take photographs, Kirsch comes forward, Goebbels hangs the medal around his neck and offers him his hand, Kirsch pretends he hasn't seen it, Goebbels assumes he is overcome with emotion and takes Kirsch's hand with a smile, then nods to him encouragingly, indicating he should say something. Kirsch turns to the audience, the applause stops. All goes quiet. Meisel, Helene and Olga stare at Kirsch in horror, expecting him to reveal himself. Kirsch opens his mouth to speak, Helene faints, Kirsch glances at her, Helene is caught by extras and carried off.

GOEBBELS: (*smiling, to Kirsch*) All this excitement...

Goebbels again nods encouragingly at Kirsch who gazes into the audience, opens his mouth again but cannot speak, so bows briefly and steps back ashamed into the row of actors. More applause, the curtain closes slowly, Kirsch is clutching at his heart with his right hand. Goebbels bows automatically as if he were the main actor.

Dim light in the auditorium. After a while the curtain rises again. (Lights out in the auditorium, working light on stage.) Goebbels and Kirsch (still in costume) are alone on stage. Kirsch is weary and depressed, and afraid he will have a heart attack.

GOEBBELS: I've written four plays. *The Wayfarer*, *Judas Iscariot*, *Seeds of Blood* and *The Stone Guest*. All in the 1920s, these days I no longer have the time. *The Wayfarer* and *The Stone Guest* would be superb parts for you, Herr Höllrigl, I'd be honored.

KIRSCH: Huv these plays ever bin performed? [Have these plays ever been performed?]

GOEBBELS: Only *The Wayfarer*. In 1931, at the National Socialist Drama Festival. Dreadful production. Dreadful leading man. A well-meaning party comrade, tried very hard. Nauseating. I hate well-meaning party comrades. Immediately banned all my plays from being performed. One day the time will come, I thought. One day I'll find the ideal leading man. (*Looks at Kirsch.*). I'd be honored.

KIRSCH: Send me yer plays. Ah'll take a look at them. Ah'm sure we can work sumhin oot. [Send me your plays. I'll take a look at them. I'm sure we can work something out.]

GOEBBELS: Thank you, Herr Höllrigl. Is there anything I can do for YOU? Do you have a request, a wish?

KIRSCH: (*ponders, then after a while:*) There is aye sumhin, but ah dinnae like tae say. [Well, there is something, but I don't like to say.]

GOEBBELS: Out with it!

KIRSCH: There's a young lassie in the ensemble, Olga Sternberg, the one who plays Berta in *Tell*. [There's a girl in the ensemble, Olga Sternberg, the one who plays Berta in *Tell*.]

GOEBBELS: The dark-haired one?

KIRSCH: Yes.

GOEBBELS: A fine talent. What about her?

KIRSCH: Weel, her background isnae entirely in order. Her mother is racially pure, but her father's a wee bit dubious. [Well, her background isn't entirely in order. Her mother is racially pure, but her father's a bit dubious.]

Goebbels looks at him displeased.

KIRSCH: Now ye ken ye'll no find a better anti-Semite than me, Minister, when it comes to race ah'm a real hardliner. It's jest that she's such a guid actress and a verra loyal National Socialist. [Now you know you won't find a better anti-Semite than me, Minister, when it comes to race I'm a real hardliner. It's just that she's such a good actress and a very loyal National Socialist.]

Goebbels looks at him, then makes a rapid decision, hunts for a piece of paper, finds one, pulls out a fountain pen and directs Kirsch to bend over so that he can write against his back.

GOEBBELS: WHAT was her name?

KIRSCH: Olga Sternberg.

GOEBBELS: (*writes something, then gives the paper to Kirsch*) If she always carries this with her, nothing can happen to her.

KIRSCH: Many thanks, Minister.

GOEBBELS: You're welcome, after all, we aren't inhuman. This isn't the first one of these I've written. When it comes down to it, every theater is basically a concentration camp on holiday. – So, business is over, now let's celebrate! (*Takes his arm.*) Come along, they're waiting for us.

KIRSCH: Do ah have tae, Minister? Ah'd much rather sleep. Tae bed wi' the chickens and up wi' the cows, that's me. [Do I have to, Minister? I'd much rather sleep. To bed with the chickens and up with the cows, that's me.]

GOEBBELS: Come now, Herr Höllrigl, please, you mustn't deprive us of the pleasure of your company. The party is solely in your honor.

Helene enters, dressed in her most seductive outfit.

GOEBBELS: Leni! You persuade Herr Höllrigl to come with us.

HELENE: (*completely hysterical*) Absolutely, absolutely! You must, Herr Höllrigl!

KIRSCH: Aye, well, for a wee while, then. [Oh well, for a little while, then.]

GOEBBELS: (*looks at the two of them*) What a couple! What a couple! I shall have a screenplay written specially for you. (*He has a sudden idea.*) Andreas Hofer, the liberator of Tyrol! What do you say to that, Herr Höllrigl?

Helene laughs nervously, Goebbels looks at her in some irritation.

KIRSCH: Aye, ah'd like tae play Andreas Hofer. His wife wiz always true tae him. That'd be a guid part for you, Frau Schwaiger. [Yes, I'd like to play Andreas Hofer. His wife was always true to him. That'd be a good part for you, Frau Schwaiger.]

HELENE: Oh, that would be wonderful! Wonderful! I'd love to! I just ADORE acting in peasant costume!

GOEBBELS: Well, let's discuss it at the party. I'm a great one for dreaming up projects! We'll soon have the whole film cast!

He takes Helene's arm, they go to the right, then come to a sudden halt because Polacek is staggering drunkenly onto the stage, dragging Eder, who is trying to hold him back, after him.

POLACEK: Propaganda Mister! Mister Propaganda man!

Three of Goebbels' SS guards appear, seize hold of Polacek and try to drag him off. He grabs hold of anything he can find, trying to resist them.

POLACEK: Mister Propaganda! It's a trick! Don't let him fool you!

GOEBBELS: (*letting go of Helene*) What does he want?

POLACEK: (*pointing at Kirsch*) He's a Jew! He's a Jew!

Helene freezes in horror.

GOEBBELS: (*to Kirsch*) Do you know this man?

KIRSCH: Aye, ah ken him. Polacek. An actor. He's no quite aw there (*taps his forehead*). Because he looks so Jewish. It's muddled his heid. He even said ye were a Jew once. [Yes, I know him. Polacek. An actor. He's not quite all there (*taps his forehead*). Because he looks so Jewish. It's muddled his head. He even said you were a Jew once.]

GOEBBELS: What? Me?

KIRSCH: (*nods*) Poor devil.

GOEBBELS: (*to the SS guards*) Get him sectioned into a secure unit.

The SS guards drag Polacek off. Eder withdraws, satisfied.

POLACEK: He's a Jew! He's a Jew!

GOEBBELS: Really, some people.

Goebbels takes Helene's arm and starts to exit with her. At this moment Kirsch has a heart attack, he groans and doubles up. Goebbels lets go of Helene to support Kirsch.

HELENE: Arthur! (*Puts her hand to her mouth.*)

GOEBBELS: (*Who hasn't heard her*) Herr Höllrigl! What's the matter?

KIRSCH: Ah'm aw right, ah'm aw right! [I'm all right, I'm all right!]

GOEBBELS: Your heart?

Kirsch nods.

GOEBBELS: It was all a bit much for you, eh?

KIRSCH: Ye could say so. [You could say so.]

GOEBBELS: You should take more care of yourself. Do you need a doctor?

KIRSCH: Naw, naw, ah'm aw right now. Ah'll jest get changed, meet me by the stage door. [No, no, I'm all right now. I'll just get changed, meet me by the stage door.]

Kirsch exits, the others watch him go. Goebbels looks around, then pulls Helene over to the door. He tries to kiss her, she pushes him away.

HELENE: Minister, this is hardly the place!

GOEBBELS: Joseph! Just call me Joseph!

She laughs hysterically, he kisses her. Curtain.

SCENE 7

The curtain rises, no set. A few chairs. Meisel, Helene, Olga and Morovitz. All are in ordinary clothes. Morovitz is still deeply insulted, Olga looks pleadingly at Helene.

HELENE: It is him, Gernot! Surely I can recognize my own husband!

MEISEL: It was a put-up job to get rid of Strassky! A bit of theater, nothing more!

MOROVITZ: I don't believe you! I don't believe you! You're trying to make a fool of me! You're all trying to make a fool of me!

They all sigh and fall silent. After a while Kirsch comes in, tired and bowed. Meisel hurries over to him and squeezes his hand.

MEISEL: Thank you! Thank you, Herr Kirsch, I'm indebted to you! I nearly passed out when you opened your, when you started! But you couldn't bring yourself to, eh?

KIRSCH: I was too much of a coward. I'd waited so long for this moment. And then I was just too cowardly. (*Laughs despairingly*.) The greatest cultural-political triumph of the German Reich! And I helped them achieve it!

Morovitz is utterly bewildered. Helene comes over to Kirsch and hugs him comfortingly. After a while Kirsch frees himself, strokes her cheek, pulls out Goebbels' piece of paper and gives it to Olga. She reads it, can hardly believe it, then shrieks with joy and hugs Kirsch.

OLGA: (*reads out the note*) I hereby declare the actress Olga Sternberg to be an honorary Aryan. Dr. Joseph Goebbels.

She shrieks with joy again, then hugs Morovitz who is standing there as if turned to stone.

MEISEL: (*sighing*) Right, back to business: *Faust*.

KIRSCH: (*shaking his head*) It's over, Herr Meisel. I've only come to say goodbye.

MEISEL: (*stares at him in shock; then*) You're very tired, Herr Kirsch, I do understand, but, what can I do, personal request by the Minister, *Faust* next, you were there.

KIRSCH: It can't go on!

MEISEL: He promised me twice the usual subsidy, how can I –

HELENE: I don't understand, Arthur! You'll be the biggest star in the German Reich!

KIRSCH: Oh, Helene... (*To everyone:*) The show is over. (*Suddenly angry:*) Over! It's time you realized that! I hate this Tyrolean monster I've turned myself into! I hate him!

Everyone stares at him. Eder appears upstage and gestures urgently at Kirsch, who goes to Helene and kisses her on the cheek, nods at the others and then goes over to Eder. They exit together.

OLGA: (*to Morovitz*) Do you believe me now, you silly ass?

Morovitz can't answer, the situation is too much for him.

MEISEL: Well! So that's that! Farewell then, my beloved theater, my blessing and my curse, my heart's blood! Come on then, we must, a run for it, our only hope!

They all stare at him, no one moves.

MEISEL: You don't seem to understand, when they find out, once they get hold of HIM, we're all doomed! Everyone follow me under the stage, the secret tunnel, we'll, quick, as fast as you can!

Meisel goes off quickly, the others hesitate uncertainly, the two Gestapo officers come on with Strassky (in handcuffs) and Polacek (in a straitjacket).

FIRST GESTAPO OFFICER: Stop right there!
Meisel stops, shocked, and turns around.

STRASSKY: Where is he?

MEISEL: Who?

STRASSKY: Don't ask stupid questions, Meisel! Our friend from Tyrol!

MEISEL: He's just coming, I expect, I assume. We're about to rehearse *Faust*.

POLACEK: Jew nose won't be rehearsing anything! Coon face! (*Laughs hysterically*.)

STRASSKY: (*to the First Gestapo Officer*) Get on with it! (*Indicates Olga.*)

FIRST GESTAPO OFFICER: Olga Sternberg, you're under arrest!

He gestures to the second Gestapo officer who pulls out a pair of handcuffs, goes up to Olga and takes her roughly by the hand. She waves Goebbels' piece of paper under his nose, he is about to push it away, then recognizes the signature and freezes. The First Gestapo Officer goes over, tears the paper out of Olga's hand and reads it, starts in horror and gives it back.

FIRST GESTAPO OFFICER: Apologies, Fräulein Sternberg!

STRASSKY: What's that supposed to mean, may I ask?

FIRST GESTAPO OFFICER: I warned you, Strassky, I told you to watch it! If you show me up one more time you're in big trouble!

Höllrigl (the real one) comes on from backstage, in clothes and appearance he is identical to Kirsch. They could be twins.

POLACEK: There he is! The nigger! The kike! The coon! The sub-human...

FIRST GESTAPO OFFICER: Herr Höllrigl, I'm very sorry but I'm afraid I must examine you.

HÖLLRIGL: Whit? [What?]

FIRST GESTAPO OFFICER: There have been a number of reports that you are in fact the Jew Arthur Kirsch.

Helene starts to sway, she clutches at Meisel for support.

HÖLLRIGL: Och aye? Who made these reports? [Oh yes? Who made these reports?]

FIRST GESTAPO OFFICER: Herr Polacek, Herr Strassky and an anonymous informant.

HÖLLRIGL: Oh aye? [Oh yes?]

FIRST GESTAPO OFFICER: Yes, I'm afraid so. We rang the Tyrolean army HQ. According to the medical certificate from your 1914 recruitment papers you have a scar on your left knee.

HÖLLRIGL: Is that so?

FIRST GESTAPO OFFICER: I would like to have a look at your left knee.
Höllrigl pulls his trouser leg up above his knee, the First Gestapo Officer goes over, kneels down and examines the knee. Helene faints and

is caught automatically by Meisel, who continues to stare spellbound at "Kirsch" and the Gestapo Officer. The First Gestapo Officer finds a scar, touches it to check that it's real, then pulls out a magnifying glass and examines it.

POLACEK: Jew knee! Jew knee! Coon legs!

The First Gestapo Officer gets up and looks grimly at Strassky, who goes over and kneels down in front of Höllrigl's knee. Unable to believe what he sees, he touches the scar, then licks his fingers and tries to rub it off.

FIRST GESTAPO OFFICER: (*yells*) Strassky!

Strassky gets up, defeated. Helene comes round and frees herself from Meisel, looking bewildered.

FIRST GESTAPO OFFICER: That's enough! First you engage in sexual relations with a racial inferior – begging your pardon, Fräulein Sternberg – and then you try to blacken the name of the greatest actor in the German Reich! (*To Höllrigl:*) I'm ever so sorry, Herr Höllrigl, I really do apologize.

HÖLLRIGL: Dinnae fash yersel'. [Don't worry about it.]

Polacek flings himself at Höllrigl's knee and bangs his forehead against it repeatedly.

POLACEK: Death to the kike! Death to everybody!

The Second Gestapo Officer yanks him up brutally and hauls him off.

POLACEK: I'll be revenged on the whole pack of you!
The First Gestapo Officer shoves Strassky's shoulder with his hand and then kicks him.

FIRST GESTAPO OFFICER: Heil Hitler, Herr Höllrigl. No hard feelings!

Höllrigl says nothing but raises his hand in a relaxed Nazi salute. The two Gestapo Officers exit with Strassky and Polacek. Olga breathes a huge sigh of relief and kisses Goebbels' piece of paper, Helene totters over to a chair and sits down, Meisel pulls out his bottle of pills, opens it with trembling hands and spills the pills everywhere but manages to stuff a couple into his mouth.

MOROVITZ: I knew you were real, Herr Höllrigl!

HÖLLRIGL: Oh aye? [Oh yes?]

MOROVITZ: (*to Olga*) It's all over between us, over! You can marry your precious Dr Goebbels for all I care!

Morovitz starts to exit and freezes. Kirsch enters from upstage. Höllrigl holds out his arms and they embrace. Meisel stares at the two of them and stuffs a couple more pills into his mouth.

HÖLLRIGL: Arthur, mon, ah've bin worried sick aboot ye! [Arthur, I've been worried sick about you!]

They look at each other.

KIRSCH: Yer lookin' well, Benedikt. [You look well, Benedikt.]

HÖLLRIGL: Aye, but ye've lost a wee bit o' weight. (*Embraces him again.*) That wiz a crazy idea of ours, wiz it no? [Yes, but you've lost weight. (*Embraces him again.*) That was a crazy idea of ours, wasn't it?]

KIRSCH: It was. Your craziness and my idea!

MOROVITZ: (*goes over to Olga*) Olga!

Morovitz tries to hug Olga, she boxes his ears, then hugs him, goes over to Kirsch and kisses him on the cheek, then takes Morovitz by the hand and exits with him.

HÖLLRIGL: Are ye comin' too? [Are you coming too?]

KIRSCH: Yes, please, if I may. How are the children?

HÖLLRIGL: Jest fine, but they miss ye, o' course. So dae I. Specially in the winter. Ah goat right grumpy wi' ma folks. Ma mother sends her love, she's deid, God rest her. [Just fine, but they miss you, of course. So do I. Especially in the winter. I got really grumpy with my family. My mother sends her love, she's died, God rest her.]

KIRSCH: I'm sorry, Benedikt.

HÖLLRIGL: Ach, when yer eighty, dying's no so hard. "Arthur can huv ma room," she said oan her deathbed. [Oh, when you're eighty, dying's not so hard. "Arthur can have my room," she said on her deathbed.]

KIRSCH: Really? The one with the view of the peak?

HÖLLRIGL: Aye, wi' the view o' the peak. [That's right, with the view of the peak.]

HELENE: (*bewildered*) I'm sorry, Arthur, I thought the children were in Switzerland?
Kirsch laughs and shakes his head.

HELENE: You mean they aren't at boarding school?

HÖLLRIGL: Och, they got enough schooling frae me. [Oh, they got enough schooling from me.]

HELENE: But, Arthur, that won't do at all, they'll run wild!

KIRSCH: No one runs wild with Benedikt around, quite the contrary.

EDER: (*comes over*) Time's up. There'll be a car waiting for you outside, Herr Kirsch, it'll be 'ere any minute. (*To Höllrigl:*) And you'd better go back by train. I'll show you the way out.

HÖLLRIGL: (*shakes Helene's hand*) Farewell, Frau Kirsch. Yer husband's a rare find, ye don't get many o' them to the pound. Ah hope ye ken that. (*To Kirsch:*) See ye this evening, Arthur. [Farewell, Frau Kirsch. Your husband's a rare find, you don't get many of them to the pound. I hope you know that. (*To Kirsch:*) See you this evening, Arthur.]

KIRSCH: (*joyfully*) Aye, ah'll see ye this evening. [Yes, see you this evening.]

Höllrigl exits with Eder.

KIRSCH: Herr Meisel, I resign.

MEISEL: I accept, with pleasure, a millstone has fallen from my, I could jump for. With your consent, I shall tell the press and the Minister that you were so consumed by debilitating homesickness that you were no good for anything, stricken with melancholy and so forth, all right? (*Shakes Kirsch's hand.*) Honored to have worked with you, Herr Kirsch. (*Goes off hastily, muttering:*) My poor suffering theater, what will become of you, how will you, but no, no, we'll get through, I'll get you through, you've survived other blows of fate, you'll survive this, too...

Helene hugs Kirsch.

KIRSCH: Goodbye, Helene. Forgive me for making a drama out of it all.

HELENE: I'd come with you. But I'm an actress, Arthur, I've got to act. I can't give it up. Give my love to the children.

Kirsch nods. Helene kisses him on the mouth, starts to leave, then turns around.

HELENE: Things will settle down here. It can't go on like this. And then you'll come back and we'll be a family again.

KIRSCH: (*sadly*) I'm sure you're right.

Helene exits. Kirsch is left alone on stage. He looks around, comes to the front of the stage and looks out into the audience.

KIRSCH: (*softly and sadly, without a hint of pathos*) I am a Jew. Hath not a Jew eyes? Hath not a Jew hands, organs, dimensions, senses, affections, passions; fed with the same food, hurt with the same weapons, subject to the same diseases, healed by the same means, warmed and cooled by the same winter and summer, as a Christian is? If you prick us, do we not bleed? If you tickle us, do we not laugh? If you poison us, do we not die?

Kirsch goes slowly off. Curtain.

THE END

Editor's Note: In the version offered here, the play ends with Kirsch left to nurse a welter of painful unresolved feelings. Several other endings have been proposed, both by the author himself and by others. Some of these retain the final note of irresolution, intimating perhaps a lingering need for vengeance, while others are more conciliatory; still others assume a straddling stance. The reason for the indecision is as follows: Mitterer's original conclusion has Kirsch's two children appearing near the end to do an impromptu recital of that part of G.E. Lessing's classic German play, *Nathan the Wise,* that portrays the hero Nathan's resignation to God's will in the wake of the slaughter of his wife and children by Christians during the Third Crusade: "Doch war auch Gottes Ratschluß das!" ["Yet this too was God's decree!"] The father Kirsch looks on approvingly, thus presumably signaling his solidarity with Lessing's enlightened ideal of tolerance. This, however, caused a flap in rehearsals for the play's premier in Vienna, not surprising in the wake of the murder of six million Jews in the holocaust. Thus sprang up this spectrum of variant endings, along with Mitterer's liberal endorsement of future directors' discretion in choosing whatever ending seems appropriate to them. One could argue that the indecision weakens the play, or, conversely, that it actually strengthens it by forcing the viewer/reader to weigh carefully the human need to forgive against the equally human need to exact justice.

Doubtless out of a dramatist's concern for the welfare of his protagonist, his "literary child," Mitterer himself favors his own original conciliatory ending that leaves Kirsch at peace. This is the version published by Haymon Verlag in 1998. At its end Kirsch's daughter Lieserl, as Nathan, intones the famous lines capturing the spirit of Enlightenment ecumenism, lines Mitterer would have us take as an externalization of the father's hard-won inner harmony. Having overcome his initial torrent of dark emotions, Nathan reveals:

Three nights had I in dust and ashes lain
Before my God and wept – aye, and at times
Arraigned my maker, raged, and cursed myself
And the whole world, and to Christianity
Swore unrelenting hate.
....
But by degrees returning reason came,
She spake with gentle voice – And yet God is,
And this was his decree – now exercise
What thou hast long imagined, and what surely
Is not more difficult to exercise

Than to imagine – if thou will it once.
I rose and called out – God, I will – I will.
(IV,7; Tr. William Taylor, Project Gutenberg E-text #3820)

Finally, it also bears mention here that the present translation omits all references to Lessing's play occurring in Mitterer's original as well as to a few other German dramas not likely to be familiar to an Anglo-American audience. In some instances references to analogous English dramas have been substituted, in others not.

THE PANTHER

Translated by

Mike Lyons, Patrick Drysdale and Dennis McCort

© Mike Lyons, Patrick Drysdale and Dennis McCort, April 2010
German original commissioned for Das Theater in der Josefstadt, Vienna
©Haymon Verlag, Innsbruck–Vienna 2008, www.haymonverlag.at
Performance rights with the Österreichischer Bühnenverlag Kaiser & Co.,
Am Gestade 5/II, A-1010 Wien
© April 2010 for translation of Rainer Maria Rilke's poem, "Der
Panther," by Mike Lyons and Patrick Drysdale

*Dedicated in friendship and admiration
to the Kammerschauspieler [title for state-honored actor of renown]
Fritz Muliar on the occasion
of his 70th anniversary on the stage*

Fritz Muliar – a life for the theater

On the 15th of July, 1937, Fritz Muliar stood on a stage for the first time, in "Der liebe Augustin" no less, given in the underground cabaret of the Viennese Café Prückel. And today, in the year 2007, the legendary actor stands before us still, celebrating his 70th anniversary on the stage. He celebrates it with a play by me. This is what he wished for himself, and I feel deeply honored.

In 1990 Fritz Muliar provided me with the greatest theatrical success of my life. Under the direction of Franz Morak, he performed *Siberia* at the Vienna Academy Theater.

With such penetration and power did Muliar embody the old man who struggles for a dignified death in the nursing home that it led to an overwhelming audience uproar. The great comedian, the "portrayer of the little man," had transformed himself into the character actor he had in any case been from the very beginning. In so doing he impressively contradicted his own pronouncement that a role such as King Lear would not suit him in the slightest, "or at best in a musical version."

For he was of course playing a King Lear, an old man on the decline who is left in the lurch.

Muliar appeared in *Siberia* over 150 times, not only at the Academy Theater, but in Salzburg, Berlin and Hamburg as well.

Herewith a brief summary of his life:

Fritz Muliar is born an illegitimate child in Vienna on Dec. 12, 1919. His natural father, a Tyrolian officer in the imperial and royal army, completely neglects him and later becomes a National Socialist. By contrast, his mother, Leopoldine Stand, who works as a secretary for the Austrian

Kontrollbank, is a fervent Social Democrat. In 1924 she meets the Russian-Jewish jeweler, Mischa Muliar, and marries him. Mischa adopts little Fritz and instructs him in the Jewish faith and the Hebrew language. Thus it is to his adoptive father that Fritz Muliar is indebted for his subsequent talent for telling Jewish jokes in that inimitable way of his. And his mother's example is doubtless one reason for his remaining an avowed Social Democrat his entire life and never being shy about saying so.

In March, 1938, Mischa Muliar flees to the USA to escape the Nazis.

Fritz Muliar is drafted in April, 1940, tours France with a theater group to entertain the troops and cracks jokes along the way about Hitler and his henchmen. He is condemned to death for "the undermining of military morale" and activities in support of the reconstitution of a free Austria. However, after seven months' detention his sentence is reduced to five years' imprisonment. To avoid such an extended term he volunteers for a penal company bound for Russia.

After the war Muliar begins as an announcer for Radio Klagenfurt, but soon heads off to Graz as an actor and director, returning to Vienna in 1949. At first he appears at the Raimund Theater; from 1952 to 1965 he performs at the Cabaret Simpl along with Karl Farkas and Ernst Waldbrunn.

Finally at the beginning of the seventies comes the big breakthrough in television: *The Adventures of Good Soldier Schweik* by Jaroslav Hasek, filmed in 13 parts by ORF/ZDF under the direction of Wolfgang Liebeneiner. More than 100 films and series follow.

Fritz Muliar becomes a member of the Burgtheater, but also appears at the Volkstheater, the Josefstadt and, of course, the Salzburg Festivals.

In 1990 the professor and *Kammerschauspieler* retires amidst pomp and fanfare, but soon finds he cannot stay away, for which we are most grateful to him. Since 1994 he is again a staunch member of the Josefstadt. With his comic talent he guarantees the comedy wing of the studio theater consistently sold-out houses – just as in decades past.

His roles are numberless. No one who has seen him can ever forget him, as Sancho Panza, for instance, in *The Man of La Mancha* at the Volksoper, as Old Age in *The Farmer as Millionaire* at the Volkstheater, as Mr. Green in *The Visit to Mr. Green* at the Josefstadt, and, of course, as the pope in *The Day They Kidnapped the Pope* at the studio theater.

Ah, Fritz, it took me seventeen years after *Siberia* finally to cobble together another play for you; I hope you'll forgive me the long wait.

I am grateful to the Josefstadt director, Herbert Föttinger, for giving me the necessary push in the form of a commission to write the play. This from a man busy with five premieres in one season (Turrini, Franzobel, Barylli, Vögel, Mitterer) – there is no director heretofore who has managed that.

And it makes me happy that a second legend of the Vienna theater is involved in *The Panther*: Elfriede Ott. Hans Weigel, her life partner, discovered and nurtured me from early on, steering me in the direction of many a literary prize. Dear, revered Hans, no longer in our midst, keep your fingers crossed for us and keep an eye on us.

Felix Mitterer

THE PANTHER

CHARACTERS:

The man without a name, old
Marion Liebherr, old
Heinz, middle-aged

Scene: *living room of a late nineteenth-century house. Two windows, parquet floor, partially raised. Standard lamps. Plants. Bookshelves with lots of books. Wall-clock. Wardrobe and mirror, next to it an umbrella stand with umbrellas and a walking stick. Dining table and chairs. On the table a large, complicated jigsaw puzzle as well as a tall, slender glass vase. Settee and table, armchairs. Several TVs of varying sizes. Stereo system with record player and LPs. Various items from mail-order houses, some still in boxes. Books, newspapers, magazines and old school exercise books stacked up on the floor. Somewhere a straw hat of the kind Maurice Chevalier wore.*

As background music (beginning, middle and end) the Chevalier song, which the Man sings together with Marion:

Paris je t'aime d'amour

Ô mon Paris, ville idéale
Il faut te quitter dès ce soir
Adieu, ma belle capitale,
Adieu, non, au revoir!

Paris, je t'aime, je t'aime, je t'aime
Avec ivresse,
Comme une maîtresse!
Tu m'oublieras bien vite et pourtant
Mon cœur est tout chaviré en te quittant!

Je peux te dire
qu'avec ton sourire
Tu m'as pris l'âme
Ainsi qu'une femme
Tout en moi est à toi pour toujours
Paris je t'aime, oui! d'amour!

Paris je t'aime, je t'aime, je t'aime, je t'aime mais voyons!
Puisque j' te dis que je t'aime, allons!
Pour les caresses
De mille maîtresses

Elles m'oublieront bien vite et pourtant
Moi j'leur faisais j'me souviendrais bien longtemps
L'une après et l'une
La blonde et la brune
M'ont fait sans phrase
Goûter mille extases
J' te l'jure que je t'appartiens pour toujours,
Paris, je t'aime – et comment! – d'amour!

IMAGE 1

Late afternoon. Dull winter light through the windows. Piles of newspapers and books and on them lots of different candles – tea warmers, red grave lights, tall candles in their holders. The Maurice Chevalier song is heard, apparently coming from an old gramophone. The end of the song is followed by a short silence.

Marion comes in from the front door, leading the Man. He is limping, she supports him. She is in mourning and carrying her coat; he is unkempt, no coat.

MARION: (*quite distraught*) I am so sorry, do please forgive me. I just can't tell you how …

MAN: Don't keep on about it. That doesn't do me any good. You've shattered my shinbone.

She gets him into an armchair. He feels his shinbone, lets out a yell.

MARION: (*puts her handbag down*) May I have a look?

MAN: No, you may not!

MARION: Shall I get a doctor? Or call an ambulance?

MAN: You can call the police. I'll charge you with causing grievous bodily harm.

MARION: No, please don't do that. I don't have a driver's licence anymore.

MAN: Ha, ha, so that's the way things are. I suppose I'm not the first to be mowed down by you then?

MARION: (*takes her coat off, hangs it up in the wardrobe*) Just a scrape, really!

MAN: You shouldn't be driving at your time of life!

MARION: You popped up, as if from nowhere. Like some apparition.

MAN: An old man doesn't just pop up from nowhere.

MARION: I'm sorry. My thoughts were elsewhere. I've just come from my husband's funeral.

MAN: My condolences.

MARION: Thank you.

MAN: Good thing it wasn't me.

MARION: What?

MAN: I've got things to do before I take my final bow. Wasn't bumping off your husband enough for you?

MARION: I did *not* bump him off!

MAN: Well, never mind. (*Notices the candles.*) Nice lighting for a party.

MARION: For him.

MAN: So you want to be his guiding light then?

MARION: Sort of. Our path is shrouded in darkness.

MAN: I suppose so.

MARION: Can I offer you something? (*Picks up a bottle of mineral water.*) Water?

MAN: I'd rather have a brandy.

She brings him a brandy, he swallows it. She pours out mineral water for herself, sits down and drinks. He grabs the bottle of brandy, pours himself some more and has another mouthful.

MAN: Have you got a cigarette for me?

She fetches a lighter and cigarettes from a drawer, gives him one and lights it, puts an ashtray in front of him, sits down again, gazes at him as if he were an apparition.

MAN: Why are you looking at me like that? It gives me the creeps.

MARION: Forgive me. It's been a shock.

MAN: What shall I say? I'm the victim. Just so typical: the culprit is in a state of shock and so it's the victim who has to apologize.

MARION: But I did apologize.

MAN: That won't make my shinbone any better.

MARION: Do you want to phone your family?

MAN: No.

MARION: Why not? They may be worried about you.

MAN: They're not the worrying sort.

MARION: I can't believe that.

MAN: It's true though.

MARION: Do you have a wife?

MAN: Of course I've got a wife. Everyone's got a wife.

MARION: And she's not worried about you?

MAN: No. On the contrary. She wants to be rid of me.

MARION: Why?

MAN: No idea. I'm an easygoing fellow. Except when I'm roused. And your husband, what was he like?

MARION: We were married for more than fifty years.

MAN: That's not what I was asking.

MARION: I buried him today.

MAN: And you don't want to speak badly of him. At least not today, is that it?

MARION: I don't want to talk about my husband with you.

MAN: Have you got any children?

MARION: A son.

MAN: Just the one child?

MARION: I had lots of children, lots of wonderful children. I was a teacher. What did you do?

MAN: I was a professional too.

MARION: And what was your job?

MAN: Listen here, I'll stop asking you about your husband and you'll stop asking me about my job? Agreed?

MARION: Of course.

MAN: How about some compensation?

MARION: How much do you want?

MAN: How much will you give?

MARION: Is your shinbone really done for?

MAN: (*rubs his shinbone, groaning as he does so*) I think there are splinters of bone poking through.

MARION: I'd better call an ambulance. Otherwise I can't be responsible.

MAN: (*suddenly stops groaning*) Hold on. (*Feels again.*) Maybe it's just a bruise, but a bruised leg hurts more than a broken one. And I could tell you a tale or two about bruises.

Marion opens her handbag, looks inside, takes out 50 euros, looks searchingly at the Man, who grimaces indignantly. She looks into the bag again, looks at the piles of newspapers, walks round them, points at them, keeps shaking her head.

MAN: What's all this about? The competitions are over and done with. Listen, I don't want old newspapers, I want cash.

She spots a particular stack of papers, moves the candle on top of it onto the floor, thumbs through the papers, finds some money, brings him four 500-euro notes.

MARION: Two thousand. Is that enough?

MAN: (*pockets the money*) It's not much. The insurance companies have written me off. I have to shell out for everything.

She looks at the clock on the wall.

MAN: Are you expecting someone?

MARION: Yes, my nephew. But not for another half-hour.

MAN: You have a nephew?

MARION: Actually my husband's nephew. His brother's son.

MAN: He looks after you?

MARION: Until recently I never saw much of him. I knew little about him. Now he's always around, every day.

MAN: Well, that seems nice of him.

MARION: He manages my affairs.

MAN: All depends what you mean. Some people do have to have their affairs managed for them.

MARION: I don't. If my son were still alive, everything would be different.

MAN: Your son's dead?

MARION: Yes, car accident.

MAN: *(startled)* Car accident?

MARION: Yes, he was only nineteen.

MAN: Dreadful. It's dreadful when children die so young. They should have the decency to wait till their parents are dead. You feel guilty to the end of your days.

MARION: You're right. You never get over the death of a child.

He takes out the money and puts it on the table.

MAN: I don't want any money.

MARION: No?

MAN: There's something else I want.

She stares at him.

MAN: I'll stay with you for a few days. Till I've recovered a bit.

She stares at him, suddenly bursts into tears.

MAN: What's the matter? Is it really that bad? I'm not a monster. I eat next to nothing. A sofa is all I need to sleep on. (*Tries out the sofa next to him.*) No, that would give me back pain. Don't you have a guest room? What are you crying for? Stop it now! I don't like it when people cry for no reason. Or are you crying for your husband?

MARION: Yes, I'm crying for my husband.

MAN: So that's all right then. Go ahead and cry. My wife wouldn't cry.

MARION: Every widow cries.

MAN: Sure, crocodile tears. Then they squander the husband's pension. They rush off to the single seniors' club and make eyes at some other man.

MARION: I'd never do that. Never!

MAN: All right, I'll be frank: if I were a widower, I'd be on the lookout for another woman like a shot. We're not meant to be on our own.

MARION: No, we're certainly not. Sometimes a dog can be a help, against loneliness. But my dog is dead.

MAN: Do you or do you not have a guest room?

MARION: I do have one.

MAN: (*looks round, sees the TVs*) You like watching TV?

MARION: Another way of coping with loneliness.

MAN: As long as I'm here there'll be no television. My eyes can't stand the garish colors.

MARION: I've had all the TVs switched to black and white.

MAN: (*in amazement*) Really?

MARION: My husband couldn't stand the garish colors either.

MAN: A man after my own heart. I would have got on well with your husband.

MARION: Definitely. He was just as quarrelsome as you are.

MAN: But I'm not quarrelsome.

MARION: There's something to be said for it. The quarrelsome ones live longest.

MAN: I'm angry, that's all! It's not every day you get run over by a car. Quarrelsome! I don't have to put up with that from a complete stranger.

MARION: (*tartly*) Sorry.

MAN: By the way, you still haven't introduced yourself.

MARION: My name is Marion Liebherr.

MAN: (*holds out his hand*) Pleased to meet you, Mrs. Liebherr.

She has to move towards him, holds out her hand.

MARION: And your name is?

MAN: (*takes a furtive look at the palm of his hand where he has written down a name with a ballpoint pen*) Altmann.

MARION: Do you have a first name as well?

MAN: I'm not going to be here that long.

There is a ring at the front door. Marion looks at the clock, gets into a panic.

MARION: What's he doing here already? Please, he mustn't see you here!

MAN: Why not?

MARION: Move now. Hurry.

She pulls him up, leads him to the wardrobe and opens it.

MAN: What's all this about? I want to go to the guest room.

MARION: (*shoves him into the wardrobe*) Shut up! *(Closes the door.)*

MAN: Now I'm being stowed away! I'm not your lover boy!

Meanwhile there have been several increasingly insistent rings of the bell; now Heinz enters. His hair is jelled and he is wearing a fashionably dark pin-striped suit. He is holding the front-door key in his hand and carrying a supermarket bag.

HEINZ: (*putting down the bag*) Why didn't you open the door, Aunty? I've worn my finger to the bone pressing that bell.

MARION: Sorry, my thoughts were elsewhere.

HEINZ: I've done the shopping for you. Nothing but bargain offers.
He hands her the receipt, she pays him from her purse.

MARION: All correct, thanks.

HEINZ: (*sniffs, sees the cigarette in the ashtray*) Do you smoke? Since when have you been a smoker? I mean it's none of my business, but it's not entirely safe with all this – (*Wants to say 'paper,' looks at the piles of newspapers, sees the lighted candles.*) It's beyond belief! (*He blows all the candles out.*) Do you know how many old people burn to death in their homes? Why are you like children, you old folk. Absolutely irresponsible! The whole building could burn down!

MARION: (*having sat down, she lays out her puzzle to hide her embarrassment*) Sorry.

HEINZ: If it isn't the stove, it's the iron. There's always something to be worried about with you.

Marion seethes over the constant reproaches.

HEINZ: I've printed out (*points*) these huge signs for you. 'Switch off stove! Switch off iron! Turn off water at the washing machine! Don't leave key stuck in front door!' And where are these signs? You chuck them away. (*He has stopped blowing out the candles, sees the 2000 euros on the table.*) I'll look after this for you, there are gangs of marauding foreigners out there. (*Pockets the money, sees the bottle of brandy and the glass.*) Brandy? (*Looks at Marion.*) Okay, so it was cold at the cemetery. Or was it that man ?

MARION: What man?

HEINZ: The caretaker-woman said that you knocked a man over as you were parking the car. There's no end to it, is there?

MARION: I just nudged him a little.

HEINZ: The caretaker says you brought him into the house.

MARION: Yes, he was here. I wanted to play it safe, make sure he wasn't injured. He smoked a cigarette, drank a brandy and then left.

HEINZ: Then why did you lie to us, Aunty Marion?

MARION: What do you mean lied?

HEINZ: We wanted to pick you up. You said you would take a taxi to the funeral.

MARION: I just love driving.

HEINZ: You mustn't drive anymore, Aunty, you know that. And you mustn't tell lies either. Only children tell lies. And they're minors. And they get punished for telling lies. (*Takes her handbag, removes the car-key, laughs as he shakes his head.*) How many spare keys have you got? (*Puts the key in his pocket.*) Never mind, I've now found a buyer for your car.

MARION: So you've already found one? Has he had a test-drive yet?

HEINZ: It's all settled. He'll pay four thousand. I'll invest it for you.

Marion is upset and fiddles with her puzzle.

HEINZ: (*in a kindly tone*) Aunty Marion, you really don't need a car any longer. Where would you want to go?

She doesn't answer.

HEINZ: (*sitting down*) Now down to business. No more shilly-shallying, no excuses. Uncle Thomas is dead and buried and at long last we need to get things settled. Now please try to remember. Where is the money?

MARION: What money?

HEINZ: The money that's not in the bank

MARION: You've been to my bank?

HEINZ: Of course I have.

MARION: What gives you the right to look at my account?

HEINZ: (*reassuringly*) The court. I have been appointed to run your affairs. Have you forgotten that already?

MARION: This is monstrous.

HEINZ: And what it amounts to is this: your husband, my uncle Thomas, used to go to the bank on every fifteenth of the month and withdraw everything, your pension and his too. And you kept to the same routine once he was gone.

MARION: I don't remember.

HEINZ: At the time of the currency change you turned up at the bank with a bag full of shillings. You exchanged it all for euros and off you went.
Marion doesn't reply.

HEINZ: Aunty! The money is yours. Nobody is going to take it away from you. You can do what you like with it. Only it mustn't be left to rot. Money has to work. Money makes more money.

MARION: My money doesn't need to make more money. My money's earned a little rest.

Heinz looks at her in consternation.

MARION: I haven't got any money, Heinz, really. At least not so much as you seem to believe.

HEINZ: All right, where is it then? Have you given it to the Church? To the Society for the Prevention of Cruelty to Animals? To the starving in some drought-stricken country?

MARION: I've bought a few things by mail order.

HEINZ: I know about that. That's why you had the court order served on you.

MARION: Yes, and it was you who had it served on me.

HEINZ: Not me, Aunty. That wasn't what I wanted.

MARION: It was you who called in the court medical officer.

HEINZ: The lawyer acting for the mail-order house reported you, and the judge sent the medical officer. You didn't pay for your purchases, Aunty Marion. In spite of repeated reminders.

MARION: I seem to have lost track of things. In any case, my mailbox was broken into several times.

Heinz rummages in a box full of letters standing next to him on the floor.

HEINZ: Look, look! Reminder after reminder! (*Holds them out.*) You haven't even opened most of them.

Marion doesn't answer, fiddles with her jigsaw.

HEINZ: No matter, that couldn't account for all the money that's missing. I've worked it out. (*Points to the things littering the room.*) This stuff is all worthless.

MARION: I gave a lot to the nursing home. To get decent treatment for my husband.

HEINZ: You and your husband have been withdrawing that money for the past 20 years. Where is it? Where? I have the patience of a saint, as you well know. But there does come a time when even I will blow my top. How did I end up playing policeman here?

MARION: Sometimes I was at the spa.

HEINZ: That was covered by health insurance.

MARION: I bought myself some books, and coffee and cake, at least three times a week. I gave your wife money whenever she was short of cash for household expenses. And I gave your children presents. And I slipped them extra pocket money.

HEINZ: We're left with no choice. (*Looks around.*) We'll have to turn the whole place upside down.

MARION: You won't find anything.

HEINZ: You've got more than a million, Aunty Marion. A million or more at least. I'll tell you what: I'll invest part of it profitably for you and with what's left you can get yourself comfortably settled in a nursing home for the elderly. Then you won't be so lonely.

MARION: If I could move in with you, I wouldn't be so lonely.

He looks at her.

MARION: I prefer to have younger people around me, you know.

HEINZ: My wife doesn't want that, Aunty Marion.

MARION: I could look after the children. Help them with their homework.

HEINZ: The computer looks after them. The play station. They both react with lightning speed; they could fly a jet fighter. If they go on showing me so little respect, I'll send them into action.

MARION: I could cook for you.

HEINZ: You cook like a peasant woman. Far too much stodgy food, far too much fat. I can't stand that. And the children are getting really chubby.

MARION: My husband always enjoyed my cooking.

HEINZ: You really don't need to be standing over a hot stove at your age. Take things easy. Enjoy these last few years.

Marion stares straight ahead.

HEINZ: Mind you, if you tell me where the money is, then I might be able to persuade my wife. I could tell her you'll be paying some rent and helping a bit with the mortgage.

MARION: I know nothing about any money, Heinz.

HEINZ: Then I fear we're in deep trouble, Aunty Marion. At your very first check-up the court medic wanted to have you registered as a dementia case.

MARION: I'm not demented!

HEINZ: Of course not. I talked him out of it. But if he finds out about the money business… I don't like having to say this, but he'll have you put in a home. Certainly not into a residence for the elderly.

MARION: What kind of age are we living in? An old person is entitled to be a bit forgetful! That's no reason to be put in a home!

HEINZ: Did you act any differently in the case of Uncle Thomas?

MARION: That's not the same thing!

HEINZ: I'm not competent to judge! The last time I saw him I was still a kid. Even then he seemed to me as old as the hills.

MARION: I'll give some thought to where the money might be.

HEINZ: Please be so kind. (*Stands up, moves away, turns round.*) Would you like to spend a few days with us? It would be a nice break for you.

MARION: No, thanks, it's all right. I buried my husband long ago, not today.

HEINZ: (*begins to leave, turns round*) I'll send someone round to get rid of this waste paper.

MARION: The newspapers stay where they are! I haven't read them all yet!

HEINZ: Don't be childish, Aunty. The sweep has told me he'll call in the fire department if the papers don't disappear soon. (*Leaves the flat.*)

Marion stares straight ahead. The Man knocks impatiently on the door of the wardrobe, at first she doesn't hear, he thumps more impatiently, she goes there, opens the door, helps him out of the wardrobe. He's not limping any more; she doesn't notice.

MAN: May I now be told why I was bundled into the closet?

MARION: I don't know, I was sort of acting on impulse.

MAN: An odd kind of impulse. Do you do that to all your visitors?

MARION: I don't have any visitors. Apart from my nephew.

MAN: Make sure you don't tell him where the money is. Otherwise you'll be in a home within hours.

MARION: I haven't got any money. Honestly.

MAN: Good, just stick to your guns. Give him a few euros now and again. Without saying where they come from. Now then, standing in a closet makes a man hungry. Will you be cooking us something nice, Frau Liebherr?

MARION: It would be a pleasure. Provided you like fatty food.

MAN: Nothing but!

MARION: (*picks up the shopping bag*) Come on then, I don't like being in the kitchen by myself.

He goes towards her, she sees that he's not limping, he immediately starts limping again, groaning as he does so.

MARION: (*pointing towards the umbrella stand*) Look, there's a walking stick there.

MAN: I don't need a walking stick. I hate sticks. If you get a stick, it only takes you one way, the way to the grave.

MARION: A hill-walker has a stick too.

MAN: I don't aspire to higher things. Am I Zarathustra?

She stares at his clothing.

MARION: But you should change your clothes, it looks like you've slept in those.

MAN: True. Left in too much of a hurry. No time for packing.

MARION: I think you're the same size as my husband.

MAN: I'm not going to put on a dead man's clothes.

MARION: As you wish. But you're due for a bath.

MAN: I'd love a hot bath. I've got chilblains from being out there in the icy cold.

The two of them disappear into the kitchen.

The Chevalier song is heard.

IMAGE 2

Night. Light from the street lamps comes through the windows. The candles are burning again.
The Man (dressed as before) wanders around among the stacks of newspapers, books and cardboard boxes.

MAN: (*mutters, sometimes incomprehensibly*) His eyes, his eyes, now weary of the passing bars at last, so very weary ... To him it seems, it seems a thousand bars, a thousand bars ... behind them there's no world? Or? His gliding gait, his gliding gait! His gliding gait ... his lithe and potent trot ...! (*Laughs bitterly.*) ... rotating in a microscopic round, damn it! Is like, is like a power-dance ... power ... power ... around a central spot, at which a mighty will made numb, numb, numb ...! The curtain ... from time to time the curtain of the eye quietly ... is quietly raised ... (*Looks into the wardrobe mirror.*) An image then appears ... (*Anguished:*) An image then appears ... An image then appears ...! (*He pulls the walking stick out of the umbrella stand, smashes the mirror with it, sits down on a stack of newspapers. In torment:*) I can't stand it. I can't stand it any longer!

During the last utterances Marion has appeared as a dark shadow and comes to a standstill. Now she approaches him. She is dressed as before. She helps him to his feet, leads him to his room.

The Chevalier song is heard.

IMAGE 3

Morning. The candles are burning. Marion leads the Man in, he's not limping. Both are dressed as before.

MAN: What happened?

MARION: You ran straight into my car.

MAN: No wonder I'm feeling so lousy. As if I'd been put through a cement mixer.

She sits him down.

MARION: You picked on me. You did it on purpose, got yourself run over.

MAN: Pardon? Got myself run over? Did it on purpose? Do I look suicidal? Only young people kill themselves.

MARION: (*rolling up his trouser leg*) That's nothing! Nothing! I knew it all along!

MAN: Leave my leg alone! Have you got X-ray eyes or something? Anyway, I fell on my head. I have a cranial trauma.

MARION: You staggered straight into a parked car, that's all.

MAN: I need a brandy.

MARION: It's eight in the morning.

MAN: Eight in the morning?

MARION: And you haven't had your breakfast. Breakfast is a must.

MAN: Sorry, I'm in a state of shock. It's not every day you get run over.

MARION: That was yesterday. By now the shock should be wearing off.

MAN: This place is a pigsty. It's incredible.

MARION: You can leave the pigsty whenever you like.

MAN: (*staring at the newspapers*) Have I been in this flat before?

MARION: You tell me.

MAN: Definitely not. I wouldn't put up with a dump like this for five minutes. (*Kicks over a pile of newspapers.*) That's all ancient history.

MARION: That's our lives. Yours too, my dear.

MAN: I'll trouble you not to be familiar with me. My life is definitely not part of that pile. Might I at least have a cigarette?

MARION: Not without breakfast.

He has a look round, sees the pack of cigarettes, picks it up. Marion takes it away from him.

MARION: Not without breakfast.

MAN: All right. In that case I'll be on my way.

He gets up, goes to the door, she follows him, crossly gives him back the pack of cigarettes. He sits down, lights a cigarette.

MAN: Good grief! (*Stubs out the cigarette.*) You're a real spoilsport. My wife was just the same. All the time. I'm well rid of her.

MARION: Is she no longer alive?

MAN: How should I know? I haven't seen her for ages.

MARION: You're divorced?

MAN: There is no divorce. It's just not done.

MARION: So you're living apart?

MAN: You could put it that way.

MARION: Your memory plays tricks on you, doesn't it?

MAN: I haven't been the same since you knocked me down.

Silence for a while. She fiddles with her puzzle.

MAN: How's your state of health?

MARION: Excellent.

MAN: You rarely hear that from old people.

MARION: Of course there's the knees, the back, the cervical vertebrae, the hammer toes ... My memory's failing ... Otherwise I'm as fit as a fiddle. How about you?

MAN: What are you supposed to say when you've just been rammed by a car?

She smiles indulgently.

MAN: It's not much fun being old.

MARION: We could go to a café.

MAN: Good idea. I could look at women. Young women. When your skin is old, their young, velvety skin drives you crazy. It's enough just to look. In the summer they're scantily clad.

MARION: It's winter.

MAN: Then I'd rather stay at home. Anyway, I can't stand that babble of voices.

MARION: I often used to go out for coffee with my girlfriends. It's nice just to chat. About this and that.

MAN: I know, you chat about your late husbands.

MARION: Whatever. Nowadays I hardly ever go to the café. Being alone in one is almost as unbearable as being at home on your own. You watch yourself eating a slice of cake.

MAN: Have you fallen out with your girlfriends?

MARION: They're all dead or in the old folks' home.

MAN: Mine are definitely still alive. They're all much younger than I am. But I don't know what's become of them.

MARION: Your lady friends?

MAN: Correct.

MARION: You were an unfaithful husband?

MAN: Somewhat unfaithful.

MARION: Did your wife know?

MAN: I expect so. Women always know everything.

MARION: That wasn't nice of you.

MAN: I'm not nice. What I mean is that when I got home, after seeing the other woman, I was always very nice to her. Maybe that's why she put up with it.

MARION: And what about her? Was she faithful?

MAN: I think so. That would've been my advice to her.

MARION: Really it might be better if you did leave now.

MAN: But my conscience has always plagued me.

MARION: Didn't you hear me? I want you to go.

MAN: Where should I go then?

MARION: Back to where you came from.

MAN: I'm not going back to where I came from. It's not nice there.

MARION: You've nothing else to say about your wife then? Beyond advising her to have been faithful? What sort of husband are you?

MAN: (*after a pause*) I'm afraid I wasn't a good husband. What more can I say? But she can put her mind at rest. I've forgotten all the blissful moments. All gone.

She looks at him.

MAN: You know, my memory ... more and more often it plays tricks on me. Sometimes I'm quite clear in my head ... And then suddenly all that's left is shreds of memory ... Images, distorted images.... Just like bad TV reception. And somebody with the remote keeps switching the channels. But it's not me. The worst thing is when the remote switches me off. Blackout, blank screen ... At one time I could recite lots of poetry by heart. Now only bits and pieces.

MARION: I'm sorry. I'm sure it'll get better. The human brain is like an earthworm.

MAN: All that's left of me is the worm. There's nothing there to regenerate. I'm dying off at both ends. I'm very tired. I don't know the last time I had a good night's sleep. Probably ages ago.

MARION: You were up and about all night. I didn't sleep a wink.

MAN: Maybe I've got used to sleeping tablets. Do you have any?

MARION: Yes, I do.

MAN: Can I have one or two, at bedtime?

MARION: Certainly. I can't sleep without that stuff either.

MAN: What did you say your name was?

MARION: Marion Liebherr.

MAN: Thank you, Mrs. Liebherr. Dreamless sleep … Very unhealthy. But what can you do …?

MARION: Why dreamless?

MAN: Sleeping pills kill dreams.

MARION: I didn't know that, Mr. Altmann.

MAN: Pardon?

MARION: I didn't know that.

MAN: No, why are you calling me Altmann? Are you making fun of me?

MARION: That's how you introduced yourself, with that name.

MAN: Did I?

MARION: Definitely

MAN: (*looks at the palm of his hand where the name is written*) I use various names. Sometimes I get confused.

MARION: Why do you use false names?

MAN: I'm being persecuted.

MARION: By whom?

MAN: I don't know. All I know is people are constantly trying to run me over.

MARION: I didn't try to run you over!

MAN: You're an exception. In your case it wasn't an intention but a lack of concentration due to hardening of the brain arteries. What time does your husband actually get home? I don't want any trouble.

MARION: My husband died a week ago.

MAN: My condolences.

MARION: Thank you.

MAN: Did you see him again? I mean when he was dead.

MARION: No. I didn't want to.

MAN: Why not?

MARION: I had already seen so many lifeless husks ... My father, my mother, three brothers and sisters and my son ... I wanted to keep the memory of my husband as a living person. He was so full of energy. So full of zest for life. At the same time lithe ... like a panther.

MAN: Like a panther! What nonsense! I've never heard a more nonsensical comparison!

MARION: If you had known him you would agree with me. And he had such a fine sense of humor. Goodness me, the laughs we had together! Admittedly, the older he got, the more spiteful his humor became. Cynical. Sometimes hurtful. In that respect you are just like him.

MAN: I've no sense of humor at all. Never did have. At all events I can't recall having one. Come now, when was I ever cynical at your expense?

MARION: He was as little aware of it as you are, Mr. Altmann.

MAN: (*about to fly into a rage but has second thoughts; then:*) Was he ill for a long time?

MARION: A very long time.

MAN: Hospital?

MARION: Nursing home.

MAN: You wanted to be rid of him?

MARION: What right have you to speak to me like that?

MAN: Sorry.

Silence.

MAN: What sort of job did he have?

MARION: He was a teacher too. A professor of literature. (*Points to the piles of books and newspapers.*) That's all his.

MAN: So it's not yours?

MARION: No, it's all his.

MAN: Why haven't you thrown this junk away?

MARION: It's not junk.

MAN: It's wastepaper. It has to go. (*He kicks over a pile, bends down to pick up a bank note.*) There's money here.

MARION: Oh, my God, and he said he would be sending someone to clear out the paper! (*She kneels down, blows out the candles and starts looking for money in the piles of newspapers.*)

MAN: Who said that?

MARION: My nephew Heinz! (*She finds some money, puts the bank notes and bundles on the floor.*)

MAN: Why do you stuff your money in between newspapers?

MARION: I've already had three con men in the flat. And so now and again I've been putting the odd note or two … (*She finds more and more money, whole bundles of it.*) No, my goodness me! How is this possible?

MAN: It mounts up over time.

MARION: My husband! That can only have been my husband! Please help me, Mr. Altmann!

The Man removes the candle from a stack of newspapers and sits on them, starts looking distractedly for money, finds some, flings it down carelessly. Right at the bottom of a pile Marion finds a savings-book, looks at it.

MARION: Oh, that was ages ago. My husband opened the account, I suppose. (*She puts it with the bank notes, continues her search.*)

MAN: That's why you didn't throw the papers away. That's your safe.

MARION: They remind me of my husband, that's why I didn't throw them away.

MAN: Very commendable. But now you need to find a fresh hiding-place. I would advise you to open a bank account.

MARION: Can't be done! I'm no longer allowed to manage my own affairs. My nephew has power of attorney. Please look after it! Please!

MAN: Why would you trust me? I'm a stranger with an assumed name.

She scoops up the bank notes and savings book, goes to him, stuffs the lot in his coat and trouser pockets, keeps a few notes, puts them in her pocket. Suddenly Heinz comes in (in a smart business suit), front-door key in one hand, brief-case in the other. He looks at the Man in astonishment.

HEINZ: And who are you?

MARION: You've got some cheek. Kindly ring first!

HEINZ: Sure. Please, who are you?

The Man stares at him.

HEINZ: Have you been struck dumb or something?

The Man reaches into the inside pocket of his coat, pulls out his ID and in so doing draws out some of the bank notes.

MAN: I really do need to get myself a wallet again. The money I've already lost ...

He hands Heinz the ID. The latter takes it in astonishment.

HEINZ: I didn't mean it like that. I'm not from the police.

MAN: I ask everyone I meet for some form of identification. On principle. These days you can't be too careful. There are crooks and con artists everywhere.

HEINZ: You're certainly right about that. (*Reads from the ID.*) Doctor George Altmann. *Looks at the photo, looks at the Man.*) The photo is a tad ancient, isn't it?

MAN: I know. I wouldn't get past an immigration control with it. But I'm not going to be leaving the country again.

HEINZ: (*hands back the ID.*) You're visiting my aunt, Doctor Altmann?

MARION: Doctor Altmann was a friend of your uncle.

HEINZ: I see. What sort of doctor are you?

MAN: Psychiatrist.

HEINZ: Ah, the Oedipus Complex! Kill your father, marry your mother!

MAN: Precisely.

HEINZ: Penis envy.

MAN: You really know your stuff. Do you work in this field too?

HEINZ: No, my business is with matters of substance. I'm in finance. Investment consultant.

MAN: So you handle paper money then?

HEINZ: But not as a consultant.

MAN: So what's so substantial about that?

HEINZ: (*sees the papers lying around*) What's going on here?

MARION: The two thousand pounds you took charge of yesterday, for safekeeping so to speak, were lying around in old newspapers. And I thought to myself there could be more. I'm getting a bit forgetful.

HEINZ: And?

MARION: Sadly, there isn't.

HEINZ: Excuse me, Doctor Altmann, I have to talk to my aunt. It's important.

MAN: Please, carry on.

He sits down, Heinz looks at him, clearly angry.

MARION: I think it's a good idea for there to be a witness, Heinz.

HEINZ: A witness? What's the point?

Marion gestures for him to sit down, he does so, she too sits down.

MARION: As a matter of fact, I do have money, Heinz. Quite a lot.

HEINZ: (*joyful*) That's what I like to hear! So in the end you did remember! And where is it?

MARION: I've given it to someone I trust for safekeeping. He'll manage it for me.

HEINZ: Oh, indeed? And who is this person?

MARION: I'd rather keep that to myself.

HEINZ: Well now, how shall I put it …? There's a will, Aunty. Uncle Thomas's. Deposited with a lawyer.

MARION: Yes, and?

HEINZ: You're the sole heir. But … I, so to speak, am your legally appointed representative, Aunty, awkward as this is for me. I manage your money. So now, please give me the name of this person of trust. Otherwise … you know, sadly … I'd be unable to do anything more for you.

MARION: Here's an amicable suggestion. You get two thousand per month from me. And in return you leave me in peace.

Heinz looks at her, struggles with himself, starts crying. They look at him in amazement.

HEINZ: (*through his tears, to the Man*) Go away. Leave the flat at once!

MAN: I can't do that. Mrs. Liebherr needs moral support now that her husband has died.

HEINZ: This is the first time I've ever cried in front of a man! I feel so ashamed!

MAN: Don't try to fight it. I've cried too. On the battlefield. And with lots of men looking on. Mind you, most of them were dead.

HEINZ: (*lets out a sob*) I too find myself on a battlefield! The stock-exchange is my battlefield. And my enemy is money! It does as it likes! It's killing me! I hate money! I hate it!

MARION: What's happened, Heinz?

HEINZ: I'm broke, I'm ruined, my investors are hounding me, threatening to report me …!

MARION: Have you been taking wild risks?

HEINZ: *They* wanted me to take the risks. My investors wanted that, they demanded it of me! And for the first few years the yields were sensational! But then, one stroke of bad luck after another. Descent into the abyss!

MARION: You're trying every trick in the book, aren't you, Heinz? You think that fleecing an old lady is child's play.

Heinz stares at her.

MARION: You are a desk clerk in your bank. You're no investment consultant.

HEINZ: Of course I am!

MARION: Your wife is always complaining to me about your still being a desk clerk at your age.

HEINZ: So behind my back you're in touch with my wife?

MARION: No. Behind your back she's in touch with me.

HEINZ: I don't do it in the bank. I do it at home, privately, on the computer. For a few special customers of the bank.

Marion and the Man stare at him.

HEINZ: The bank mustn't know. But I'm smart, I really am! She always thinks I'm useless. I've had it up to here. I'm going to get a divorce.

MARION: Your wife has been thinking that way for quite some time!

HEINZ: I beg you, Aunty. Let me have the money! Otherwise I might as well kill myself!

MARION: Even if you put me in a home I still won't tell you who has the money. And I won't tell any lawyer, judge or medical officer either. (*She pulls out some money and lays it on the table.*) Here's another four thousand you can add to the two you had yesterday.

HEINZ: (*looks at the money*) That's chicken feed, that's nothing. You really don't need it, Aunty! You don't need a million! But I do!

MAN: She's planning a cruise on the Queen Elizabeth! A whole year, round the world. And then she's buying herself a Rolls-Royce complete with chauffeur. They don't come cheap these days. The chauffeurs, I mean.

Heinz looks at the Man in dismay.

MARION: Take it or leave it.

Heinz stares at the money, grabs it, gets up, pockets it, starts to leave, turns round.

HEINZ: Oh, by the way, Aunty Marion: that guy you ran over yesterday, he's a con man.

MARION: What makes you think that?

HEINZ: A lady client of mine was also taken in by him.

MARION: What makes him a con man?

HEINZ: He dashes out in front of a car, pretends to be hurt and gets taken into the house. He stays there for a few days, stuffs himself, boozes, smokes, behaves dreadfully, gets some compensation and then he's off again. A homeless scrounger.

MARION: Why do people fall for it?

HEINZ: It doesn't look good if you run down an old man. It can get you into hot water. Did you give him any money?

MARION: No, he didn't ask for any.

HEINZ: (*looking at the Man*) That's not you by any chance, Doctor Altmann?

MARION: He's my husband's best friend! Go now, Heinz, otherwise you won't see another penny!

HEINZ: (*suddenly sobbing*) One hundred thousand, Aunty! Just one hundred thousand!

Marion merely gives him a cool look.

HEINZ: (*turns away*) To treat your own flesh and blood like that...! To plunge an entire family into the abyss! Out of pure greed! (*Goes away, disappears.*)

MAN: (*loudly, commandingly*) Mr. Heinz!

Heinz reappears.

MAN: One more word!

Heinz stares at him.

MAN: Come closer! Step lively!

Heinz comes closer. The Man stands up, goes over to Heinz, eyes him up and down, folds his hands behind his back, walks round Heinz, much to the latter's annoyance. Marion looks on in amazement. The Man cups Heinz's chin, turns his face this way and that, scrutinizes it carefully, shakes his head.

HEINZ: (*brushes the Man's hand aside*) What's all this about?

MAN: What sort of nephew are you? Whose?

Heinz doesn't answer immediately.

MARION: My husband's brother is his father.

MAN: Indeed. I know your husband's nephews, Mrs. Liebherr. This is not one of them.

The nephew becomes uneasy. Marion looks at the Man in surprise, then she turns to Heinz.

MARION: Can you please explain this?

Heinz doesn't answer.

MARION: Are you willing to give up the two thousand a month?

HEINZ: I've never claimed to be a son of your husband's brother. You're confusing things, Aunty.

MARION: I'm not confusing anything. At the very least, that's what you led me to believe. Please stop calling me Aunty.

MAN: (*to Heinz*) Well, we're listening. And our patience is wearing thin.

HEINZ: (*to Marion*) I'm related to you on your sister's side.

MAN: (*to Marion*) This man is a con man, Mrs. Liebherr, a cheat, a swindler. Of the worst kind.

HEINZ: No I'm not! For years I've been looking after you, right from the time your husband went into the home. Selflessly! I don't deserve this treatment, Marion!

MAN: You'll relinquish your power of attorney. Of your own accord. You'll inform the court that Mrs. Liebherr is of sound mind and needs no one to act for her. And you'll never again trouble her with your presence.

MARION: Out with you! Out!

Heinz leaves the flat with his tail between his legs.

MARION: It's beyond me! He worms his way in here to swindle me! Oh, what a relief! Thank you, Thomas! Thank you for remembering.

MAN: Remembering what?

MARION: The faces of the nephews.

MAN: What nephews? I was just bluffing. How am I supposed to know your husband's relatives, Mrs. Liebherr?

MARION: I am very grateful to you, really. But now's the right moment for you to put an end to this farce, isn't it?

MAN: I'm exhausted. May I take a nap now, please?

MARION: No, you may not take a nap! I want you to put an end to this farce!

MAN: (*sits down*) Leave me in peace, please.

She looks at him.

MAN: This isn't a farce!

MARION: Actually, it is. And rather a cruel one at that.

MAN: Really? I can easily imagine someone much crueller.

MARION: Yes, I know, *I'm* cruel!

MAN: I didn't mean you.

MARION: I'll prove it to you right now, you leave me no choice. There was this young man who lost his life in a car accident.

MAN: (*tonelessly*) No. Not that.

MARION: There was no alcohol involved, it was a fine summer's day, there were no skid marks, he simply drove at top speed through the guard rail into the river.

MAN: I don't want to hear this!

MARION: So it was suicide. What was this young man's name?

The Man stiffens as if turned to stone.

MARION: Tell me! Tell me his name! And why did he kill himself?

The Man starts trembling, clenches his fists, stares straight ahead.

MARION: (*fearful for him*) I'm sorry. I'm sorry. (*Takes his hand.*) Forget it. It has nothing to do with you.

He calms down. She sits down again.

MARION: Just now I had this odd feeling. That this is my husband and he's playacting with me.

MAN: Can't be me. A play must be planned. Something I can't do. I live only in the moment. From time to time ... (*He can't remember how it goes on.*)

MARION: From time to time the curtain of the eye ...

MAN: is quietly raised … an image then appears … (*He can't go on.*)

MARION: … goes through the limbs in silence, tension high –

MAN and MARION: – and once within the heart it clears.

Stage darkens. The Maurice Chevalier song is heard.

IMAGE 4

Overcast afternoon. The place has been tidied up, the stacks of newspapers, boxes and other items are gone. The burning candles are on pieces of furniture and on the window sills.

VOICE OF MARION: (*from the entrance*) Where are you going?

VOICE OF MAN: To the café.

MARION: I cannot allow that! Come here please!

Marion leads the Man in.

MAN: Pardon, what's all this about! Am I under house arrest? Am I in quarantine?

MARION: You are injured. I knocked you over in my car.

MAN: Really?

MARION: Yes, I was going much too fast. Once your legs no longer carry you the way they used to, the urge to put your foot down is irresistible.

MAN: I remember. You came rushing straight at me. I sailed a good five yards through the air.

MARION: I saw it. Were you previously in films?

MAN: Why do you ask?

MARION: Well, it was the way you rolled over – fantastic!

MAN: Honestly?

MARION: Anyone else would've broken every bone in his body.

MAN: And his neck. Well, I wasn't a gymnast in my youth for nothing. (*He is dumbfounded at being able to remember.*) I was a gymnast in my youth!

MARION: That explains everything.

MAN: I was an ace. I won championships.

MARION: Over time the bones turn brittle anyway. (*Carefully runs her fingers over him.*) Is everything really intact?

MAN: (*waggles his arms and legs*) The extremities are in good working order.

She gets him seated.

MAN: (*feels his head*) The top of my skull would not seem to have been cracked.

MARION: A brandy?

MAN: A brandy for the shock.

She pours him one out, hands him the glass.

MARION: To your very good health, Mr. ...

MAN: (*studies the palm of his hand*) Altmann, George Altmann. (*Drinks.*)

MARION: My name is Marion Liebherr.

MAN: Pleased to meet you, Mrs. Liebherr.

MARION: A cigarette, Mr. Altmann?

MAN: My doctor has forbidden it.

MARION: One for the shock can't do any harm.

MAN: Very well then, to relax me.

She gives him a cigarette, lights it for him.

MAN: Thank you. I won't be dying of lung cancer anyway. In a car crash, more likely. (*Laughs loudly.*) Don't you think?

MARION: I think I'd better give up driving.

MAN: But not on my account! Really, it wasn't that bad.

MARION: I might even do it to someone else. Then I'd end up in front of the judge.

MAN: Generally pedestrians have only themselves to blame. They're a pigheaded lot. Old people in particular are much given to pigheadedness. They walk right across the street with the light on red. And shake their sticks at the drivers.

MARION: Thank you for being so considerate to me, Mr. Altmann.

MAN: Don't give up your car. You'd be giving up your freedom. If you've got a car you can just take off. Simply jump in and take off. And in no time you're by the sea. Or in Paris.

MARION: Oh yes, Paris. We were often in Paris.

MAN: You were often in Paris too?

MARION: Yes, with my husband, sitting on the banks of the Seine in the spring sunshine, with a bottle of red wine, with cheese and a baguette … Paradise.

MAN: Yes, paradise … Could we have seen one another there? Your face seems somehow familiar.

MARION: It's quite likely that we saw one another there. I'll have one too.

She pours herself some brandy, tops up the Man's glass, they drink a toast.

MARION: To good times in Paris.

MAN: To good times.

They drink. He begins to sing the Maurice Chevalier song, she listens to him, smiling. Sometimes he forgets the words, then she sings along to help him.

MARION: It's a long time since I last heard that ... Thanks.

MAN: So you know it too?

MARION: Of course.
They take a long look at each other.

MARION: My husband used to sing it all the time.

MAN: (*after a pause*) Where is your husband?

MARION: That's a complicated story.

MAN: Tell it to me. I'd like to know.

MARION: It was seven years ago. His memory got progressively worse, he kept mislaying things. And accusing me of having taken them. He got lost more and more often and could no longer find his way home. And in the end he could no longer recognize me. At first I suspected that he was just putting it on. To annoy me. He would call me by his mistress's name. He had a mistress for nearly twenty years, just imagine that. His earlier little flings didn't bother me. Not especially. In any case he was a good father. He liked being at home and he really loved our son. It was when the boy had his fatal accident, that it all began. He stayed away for days on end. Sometimes weeks. That was how he met his mistress. She was much younger than me. Since then, no other affairs. He was faithful to her. He was faithful to her. Do you understand what I mean? I was deeply hurt.

She is silent for a while. He watches her intently.

MARION: No, he really didn't recognize me anymore. I had to keep the flat locked because he was constantly running off. The doctor prescribed medication. He didn't take it or would spit it out when I wasn't looking. It all became more and more unbearable. Every day I went to the park with him. I had to keep a tight hold on him, like a little child. One day he broke away and ran into a car. Then it was straight from the hospital into the nursing home. The doctors insisted.

She looks at him.

MAN: I am sorry.

MARION: I visited him every day. Sometimes he recognized me and begged me to get him out.

MAN: That was asking too much.

MARION: Once I found his mistress with him. He called her by her name. And he asked her to undress and get into bed with him.

MAN: With you there?

MARION: With me there.

MAN: Outrageous behavior. If I'd been you I'd have given him a piece of my mind.

MARION: For three months I didn't go to see him.

MAN: Served him right.

MARION: After that I visited him more and more rarely. And finally not at all.

MAN: Any fair-minded person would understand that.

MARION: He *is* my husband. So come what may … stick together … in good times as in bad … I let him down. I got rid of him. Washed my hands of him. With time even his face faded more and more from my memory.

She holds back her tears. Starts to fiddle with her puzzle.

MAN: He would've got rid of you too.

MARION: Never.

MAN: Do you know what he said to me?

MARION: You knew him?

MAN: I met him playing bridge. We were in the same bridge club. "She doesn't shine my shoes anymore," he said. "I think I'll have to put her into a home."

MARION: (*laughs*) Such nonsense. I don't believe you.

MAN: "She doesn't clean the bath, nor the wash basin. In the flat it's so dusty that I'm constantly sneezing. She wants a cleaning woman, just imagine that, Doctor Altmann. Why should I pay a cleaning woman while she sits around killing time with her confounded jigsaw? Apart from that, to this very day she can't cook, that teacher-woman. The stuff she puts in front of me, incredible! But she has to have a dishwasher. Not to mention the money spent on hairdressing. And she keeps on talking while I'm reading. I think I'll stick her in the home and find myself a housekeeper. A foreign girl, not too old. And with her I'll do a round-the-world trip." That was how your husband spoke to me. So you needn't have a bad conscience, Mrs. Liebherr. He was an egotistical bastard. A tyrant.

MARION: (*almost tenderly*) Stop now. I don't like you talking about my husband in that way.

MAN: I mustn't keep you any longer. I don't want it said of me that I'm trying to settle in here. Thank you for the brandy. (*Makes as if to get up.*)

MARION: Please stay.

MAN: You want me to stay?

MARION: Please. I could do with a little company. Unless someone is waiting for you.

MAN: Not to my knowledge.

MARION: Then I'll make us some coffee. All right by you?

MAN: A nice coffee would suit me fine. Don't skimp on the beans!

MARION: I'll be back in a second.

She disappears into the kitchen. He gets up, walks about, has a look around. He comes to the smashed mirror, looks into it.

MAN: (*towards the kitchen*) The mirror is broken.

VOICE OF MARION: Has been for ages. My husband smashed it.

The Man sees the walking stick in the umbrella stand.

MAN: May I use the stick? I do still feel a bit wobbly, from my gymnastic leap.

VOICE OF MARION: Please do!

He takes the stick, tries it out.

MAN: Is this your stick, Mrs. Liebherr.

VOICE OF MARION: No, I got it for my husband. After he fell several times flat on his face. But once in a rage he threatened me with it. He came close to beating me. Then he flung it out the window. Only the window was closed.

MAN: And still you come to the defense of this loathsome creature?

VOICE OF MARION: There was more to him than that!

MAN: I do hope so. (*Has a look at the stick.*) Mind you, it's an elegant stick. Normal handle. No rubber tip … Actually, rubber tips are a pet hate of mine. And many of them have three claw-like things at the lower end – ghastly! (*He walks around with the stick.*) A completely different feeling. You feel safe. Rule number one for an old man is: don't fall over! If you fall over, you're done for. (*He walks around, looks at pictures on the walls, looks at books on the shelves. He comes to an enlarged photo which shows a couple lolling on the banks of the Seine. It's Marion and her husband when they were younger, he's wearing his Chevalier hat. The Man looks at the photograph.*) I'm just having a look at the Paris photo. You really look very happy, Mrs. Liebherr.

VOICE OF MARION: So does my husband, doesn't he?

MAN: (*looking at the husband*) Yes, he looks very happy too. Beggars belief, that sheer delight in living. Almost over the top. I was never that happy.
He has a further look around, is amazed to see the Chevalier hat, walks across, picks it up, looks at it, puts it on, starts to sing the song again, does a few dance-steps as well.

VOICE OF MARION: (*singing along in the kitchen*)

Heinz comes in with his briefcase. The Man doesn't see him, as he has his back to Heinz. Heinz watches the Man for a while.

HEINZ: (*calls*) Hey, Aunty Marion!

Startled, the Man turns towards Heinz, takes the hat off, puts it down. Marion comes from the kitchen.

MARION: You've got some nerve –

HEINZ: So he really has settled in with you! (*To the Man:*) Old man, you are about to get your comeuppance!

MARION: Doctor Altmann has not settled in with me. He is to be my guest, for a few days. And now go!

HEINZ: So, you've invited him in for a few days. Your husband's best friend! Uncle Thomas's very best friend! Am I right?

MARION: Tell me what it is you want, Heinz.

HEINZ: I'm shielding you! From your own naivety. From your own gullibility! Blood is thicker than water! You can treat me as badly as you like, you can even deny your blood-tie with me, I'll always stand by you, Aunty.

MARION: God help me! Please be so kind as to say what you have to say, and then make yourself scarce again!

HEINZ: Doctor George Altmann, my dear aunt, escaped ten days ago from a nursing home. The police are searching for him on behalf of his family.

MARION: (*to the Man*) You ran away from the nursing home, did you?

The Man sits down.

MARION: Is this so?

MAN: It's possible. Well, yes.

HEINZ: So Doctor Altmann, now I must put on my policeman hat for a moment. (*He pulls out a small folded notice, unfolds it, looks at it.*) Wanted, Doctor George Altmann, missing since blablabla ... (*To Marion:*) It's posted everywhere. (*He holds the notice under the Man's nose.*) And what do we see here? (*Points to a photo on the notice.*) What is that, Doctor Altmann?

MAN: A photo.

HEINZ: And who is this a photo of?

MAN: Me?

HEINZ: (*shows the photo to Marion*) Does the gentleman in this photo look anything like the gentleman there? (*Points to the Man.*)

MARION: Not really.

HEINZ: And what do we conclude from that, Aunty Marion?
Marion does not reply.

HEINZ: We conclude that this gentleman (*pointing to the Man*) is not Doctor George Altmann. Who are you really? What is your name?

MAN: I don't know. I was in the war. Someone put a bullet through my head.

HEINZ: You've got a screw loose, so to speak?

MAN: Correct.

HEINZ: Well now, for that there are suitable institutions. Or are you an impostor, you scruffy old fart?

MARION: What sort of language is that! Be so kind as to stop tormenting him, Heinz!

HEINZ: You keep out of this, Aunty! (*To the Man:*) Where did you get Doctor Altmann's identity card from? Well?

The Man does not answer.

HEINZ: (*getting out his cell phone*) I'm afraid I must now summon the forces of law and order.

MARION: (*to the Man*) Tell him please!

MAN: I'll tell him.

HEINZ: All right, you have my undivided attention.

MAN: I found the card.

HEINZ: He found it! Just as I thought at the start! (*Dials a number.*)

MAN: No, please don't! I'll tell you everything.

HEINZ: But don't lie! Don't lie. No more lying, old man! Or there'll be hell to pay.

The Man tries hard to concentrate.

HEINZ: (*to Marion*) The wheels are turning in that brain of his. (*Shouts at the man.*) You old shitbag! Stop looking for excuses! This is no time for reflection. A confession is called for!

MARION: A bit more respect, if you please. Okay?

HEINZ: Respect? This is the con man, Aunty Marion. This is the homeless scrounger who gets himself run over and fleeces decent people!

MARION: He has lapses of memory, give him time! Otherwise you'll learn nothing!

The Man stands up, walks around with the stick, ponders. Heinz follows right behind him.

HEINZ: Okay, take your time. All the time you need. But don't be too long.

MAN: I don't feel so good. I can't concentrate.

HEINZ: When you put me through the mill yesterday you were concentrating just fine! (*Looks at his watch.*) And now! Your time's run out! Well? Well? How about it?
Marion turns indignantly away.

MAN: I've got it, it's coming back to me! He gave me his identity card.

HEINZ: Gave it to you? Gave it to you, did he? Where then?

MAN: In the nursing home.

HEINZ: In the nursing home? Why would he give you his card? That's what I'd like to know. Then I'll be content.

MAN: He offered it to me. It was his idea.

HEINZ: His idea? No, really?

MAN: Yes, his idea.

HEINZ: But what was the point? Why? Where would he get such an idea from?

MAN: I wanted to get away.

HEINZ: Oh, so you were an inmate too?

MAN: I was an inmate too.

HEINZ: And – what happened then? Don't make me drag every single word out of you!

MAN: He was in his death throes. In a desperate struggle for life.

Heinz looks at Marion, impatiently raises his hands above his head. Marion stares at the Man. He struggles to collect his thoughts.

MAN: Now let me think … One more moment, please …

HEINZ: He's driving me up the wall! Right up the wall!

MARION: (*to the Man*) You swapped identities with him, didn't you?

MAN: Yes! That's what happened! He was lying in the room for the terminally ill. I visited him there. His belongings along with his identity card were in a cardboard box on the window seat. I sat next to him, the whole time, for hours on end. And when he was dead I pocketed the card. And I removed his chart and put mine into the folder. Then I left.

Marion and Heinz stare at him.

MAN: That is the truth.

HEINZ: And so now you've found yourself a cosy nest. And now you and my aunt are booked on the Queen Elizabeth. Outer cabin, and dance band, and gourmet cuisine. And when you get back, the Rolls Royce waiting at the dock. Am I right?

MAN: No.

HEINZ: Of course I'm right. I'm afraid I have to cook your goose for you. Because I don't like the smell of it! Not one little bit. This is my aunt, old man, who is not competent to manage her own affairs, and I won't let you pluck and draw her like a Christmas turkey! That's why I am now going to call the guardians of law and order.

Heinz dials a number on his cell phone.

MARION: (*goes to the phone*) I can do that too, you swindler!

HEINZ: (*lowers the cell phone*) Yes, do it then, report me! What better proof of paranoid dementia could there be? You'd be whisked off to the home yourself. Phone. Give it a try!

Marion becomes anxious, hesitates. Heinz dials his cell again.

HEINZ: In ten minutes you'll be behind the bars of a cot, old man. And that's one you won't escape from.

Marion goes to the Man, thrusts her hand into his pockets, pulls out bundles of bank notes, flings them in Heinz's direction. The latter lowers the cell phone, stares dumbfounded at this financial manna from heaven.

MARION: Forget what you've heard, Heinz.

HEINZ: Agreed.

MARION: I have your word?

HEINZ: You have my word of honor, Aunty. To be honest, I don't know much about these things anyway.

He kneels down, scoops up the money. The Man sits down.

MARION: Keep your word and there could be more to come.

HEINZ: No idea who this man is! Never laid eyes on him (*He fetches his briefcase, opens it, tucks the money inside.*) Oh, my God, what a great feeling this is! (S*niffs at it.*) And what a lovely smell! (*He locks the case, stands up.*) I've just won the jackpot! Dear Aunty, you won't see me for another month. No, let's say for two weeks. (*He heads for the door, disappears, reappears, waves.*) See you tomorrow, Marion! Take care! (*He leaves the flat with a howl of delight.*) Money is fabulous! I love it!

Marion looks towards the Man, who is staring straight ahead. She goes to him, sits down, looks at him. Only after a while does he raise his head and return her look. Outside it is starting to snow.

MARION: I've been wondering the whole time who I actually buried. It was Doctor Altmann, wasn't it?

MAN: I don't understand.

MARION: For you this is all just playacting. Whether planned or not. Or some devilment in you makes you play this game with me.

He looks at her helplessly.

MARION: It's a kind of revenge, am I right?

The Man looks at her, seemingly unable to understand what she means.

MARION: I've happily played my part in the melodrama, haven't I? As a kind of atonement. Can we now please put an end to it?

MAN: I don't know what you mean, Mrs. …

MARION: I couldn't put up with it if you went on in this way. I couldn't endure it. At some point this has to end.

MAN: (*ponders; after a while*) I was looking for someone. (*After a while*) My wife. My wife.

MARION: You've found me.

He looks at her, doesn't seem to know her.

MARION: Stop this nonsense or I'll put you back in the institution!

MAN: (*hesitantly*) You … are my wife …?

MARION: Yes, I am your wife.

MAN: My wife ….

MARION: What's your name?

MAN: (*thinks hard*) Liebherr.

MARION: First name?

MAN: (*stuttering desperately*) Recently, since I've been on the run, things being what they are, I've used so many assumed names. I … Please excuse me …

MARION: Thomas.

MAN: Of course, Thomas! Thomas Liebherr! Please not back to the institution!

MARION: No.

MAN: Do you promise me?

MARION: I promise.

MAN: Thank you.

MARION: But you are to promise me something too. (*He looks at her.*) To stop being so bad-tempered with me.

He feels a fit of temper coming on, controls himself.

MAN: In this condition you easily fly off the handle. I'll make an effort, I promise.

MARION: (*hugging him*) Welcome home.

MAN: (*hugging her likewise*) Thank you. Thank you, Marion.

MARION: It really is you, isn't it? I'm not fooling myself?

MAN: It is me, forgive me.

MARION: I forgive you for everything you forgive me for.

From the street the screeching of car-brakes is heard. Marion listens, goes to the window, opens it, leans out.

MARION: Oh, it's Heinz! (*She turns to the Man.*) A car's knocked him down. (*She looks out again, laughs.*) The money's sailing through the air like autumn leaves. Yes, catch it, children! Spend it all on computer games!

She closes the window again, comes back to the Man, sits down next to him, looks at him. He seems sad and lost.

MARION: I can help you. I can be your memory. We'll start with the simplest things. With lovely experiences, for example. I can tell you about our trips to Paris.

MAN: (*after a while*) I miss my poems. – The Panther. The Panther.

MARION: Now weary of those passing bars at last,
    his gaze finds nothing more that it can hold.
    To him it seems a thousand bars go past,
    behind the thousand bars there is no world.

    His gliding gait, his lithe and potent trot,
    rotating in a microscopic round,
    is like a power-dance round a central spot,
    at which a mighty will, made numb, is found.

    From time to time the curtain of the eye
    is quietly raised – an image then appears,
    goes through the limbs in silence, tension high,
    and, once within the heart, it clears.

MAN: (*after a while*) Thank you.

MARION: Rilke wrote that in Paris. In the Jardin des Plantes.

MAN: Yes, in Paris.

MARION: I'll get the coffee.

She goes into the kitchen. The Man watches her go, stares straight ahead, after a while gets up, looks around, fetches the Chevalier hat, puts it down by the vase on the dining table, reaches into his inside pocket, pulls out a red rose, puts it into the vase, looks at it, touches the blossom. The Chevalier song is heard. The Man walks with his stick towards the exit and as he passes the broken mirror looks into it.

MAN: An image then appears …

He puts the stick into the umbrella stand, takes the remaining bank notes and the savings book out of his pockets, puts everything down, looks around once more, leaves the flat. After a while Marion comes out of the kitchen carrying a tray with a coffee pot and cups, looks around searchingly.

MARION: Thomas? Where are you, Thomas? (*She puts down the tray.*) Thomas?

Marion disappears, looks for him everywhere in the flat. It grows darker. Marion reappears, sees the rose, stiffens, walks over to it, looks at it, touches it, touches the Chevalier hat, fears for the Man, walks swiftly to the wardrobe, takes out her coat, puts it on, leaves the flat to search for the Man.

VOICE OF MARION: (*echoes in the hall*) Thomas? Where are you? (*frightened:*) Thomas!

The room grows darker still. Outside there are snowflakes. The red rose glows in the vase. It slowly becomes completely dark. Music stops.

THE END

AFTERWORD

By Gerd K. Schneider

> "Despise my nation–
> We did not choose a nation for ourselves.
> Are we our nations? What's a nation then?
> Were jews and christians such e're they were men?"
> (G. E. Lessing, *Nathan the Wise*, II, v; Tr. William Taylor)

In his play, *In The Lions' Den* (1998), Felix Mitterer portrays a Jew posing as an Aryan. This sounds far-fetched but it is based on historical precedent. The play's setting is the era of the Third Reich with all the biological and racial fanaticism of National Socialism and its sympathizers against all that was considered Jewish. The Jews, so it was believed, were a parasitic slave race; they were primarily interested in money, and they were greedy. The Germans, on the other hand, and other members of the Indo-European race, possessed strength, courage and honor. They also looked different: they were slender and tall, with hair that was blond or red. According to the *Nuremberg Racial Purity Law* and the *Law for the Protection of German Blood and German Honor,* passed in 1935, Jews and non-Jews were forbidden to mingle or intermarry, and Jews were excluded from certain professions. This is the setting of Mitterer's successful play, which unmasks the ideology of this era and takes it *ad absurdum.*

The historical facts are the following: The Jewish Leo Reuß, born in Galicia, was an actor in Berlin. During a performance of Henrik Ibsen's *Hedda Gabler* in Stettin, a gang of Nazi brownshirts interrupted the performance. Because of the new Nuremberg racial laws Reuß was no longer allowed to perform on German stages. He then changed his identity by coloring his hair blond and growing a beard. With these cosmetic changes the 'Hydrogen-Aryan' returned to Vienna in 1936 as a Tyrolean mountain farmer from the Oelz valley, convincingly portraying the Nazi ideal of the earthbound Aryan, because he also spoke in native Tyrolean dialect. He had thus invented *Überlebenstheater* – theater for survival, as Hilde Haider-Pregler coined it.

At the Theater in der Josefstadt, Ernst Lothar presented a dramatized version of Arthur Schnitzler's novella, "Frl. Else," and Reuß was given the part of Herr von Dorsday, a cynical art dealer. This meant, ironically, that, in his debut performance, on December 2, 1936, he found himself playing a rich parvenu Jew, someone who believed that money could buy anything, including a viewing of the naked body of Else, a young Jewish girl whose father had gambled away his client's trust fund. Schnitzler, the author, was himself Jewish. Moreover, Jewish though Reuß was, his name was no longer Reuß: he now called himself Brandhofer, a name reminiscent of Andreas Hofer, the Swiss patriot.

Brandhofer-Reuß was an immediate success, and he received very favorable press because the Nazis had found an icon of their racial supremacy: a farmer, product of his native soil, the Tyrolean mountains, who looked every inch a member of the master race. Brandhofer's deception was discovered a week after the premiere, and the Nazis were stunned. In order to mitigate the negative publicity generated by the hoax, they allowed him to continue to work for a year under the name "Brandhofer-Reuß." He then emigrated to Paris and, in 1937, to America where he was lionized as the "man who hoaxed the Nazis." Under the name of Lionel Royce he performed in many Hollywood propaganda films, including the 1939 film, *Confessions of a Nazi Spy*. He died in 1946 in Manila.

In *Lions' Den*, composed of seven scenes, Felix Mitterer changes some of the facts for the sake of dramatic cohesion.

The protagonist is an actor, Arthur Kirsch,[1] who plays the Jew Shylock in Shakespeare's *Merchant of Venice*, a role the real Reuß never played on stage, but which gives Mitterer the opportunity to include relevant passages from this play in his own. In the wake of the interrupted performance by the organized gang of Hitler's *Sturmabteilung*, the S.A. (*Storm section*), Kirsch is forced to humiliate himself by scrubbing the stage floor, with his wife Helene looking on. She has no deep spousal or family feeling for her Jewish husband, being rather highly opportunistic and far more interested in her career as a stage and film actress than in her family life, not excepting being a mother to her young children. Nor is she above having affairs with other actors, even trumpeting her implied dalliance with Joseph Goebbels. She is also the only colleague who does not recognize Kirsch later on in the play. Kirsch disappears with his two young children. While he is away, he conspires with a Tyrolean mountain farmer to assume his identity, and returns to the stage world as Benedikt Höllrigl – presumably in Berlin, the Nazi hotbed: the "lions' den." Upon his return he "plays" a stereotypical Tyrolean mountain farmer, always carrying the official party German newspaper in his pocket and speaking in Aryan clichés the Nazis loved to hear, and these in Tyrolean dialect. In this new role he is utterly convincing to the German party members, so much so that Joseph Goebbels, the Nazi propaganda minister, suggests he take the principal part in one of his mediocre plays, as well as play Andreas Hofer, the legendary Swiss innkeeper and patriot who in the early 19th century led a rebellion against the Franco-Bavarian forces.

Höllrigl does not perform as Andreas Hofer, but as Wilhelm Tell, the legendary Swiss marksman who fought for the independence of his country. Friedrich Schiller's masterpiece is certainly to be understood as a symbol of patriotic fervor, but no less as a call to arms against the tyranny of state authority. Tell is not subversive of the authorities of the

Habsburg empire, but by the same token he refuses to bow before the hat of Gessler, who represents the Austrian ruler; indeed, he later assassinates Gessler. The renowned Swiss hero can be regarded as a symbol of the battle against political oppression and the deprivation of individual freedom. The Ruetli oath itself could be taken as an epigraph for Mitterer's play: "There is a limit to the tyrant's power." Kirsch-Höllrigl is convincing in this role as patriotic liberator and is highly lauded by the Nazi press.[2]

In some ways Kirsch-Höllrigl does succeed with his masquerade. First of all, he gets revenge for his own and his fellows' dehumanizing treatment at the hands of the Nazis. Secondly, he proves his ability as an actor. In addition, he is able to help an actress who cannot prove her Aryan background by getting her a *Persilschein* (certificate of whitewash) from Goebbels. However, he falters in his larger purpose, which is to expose the racial ideology of the Nazis publicly on stage. In the dramatic moment of his opportunity to do so, with the minister of propaganda attending the performance, he cannot summon the courage to reveal himself on stage as a Jew. He retreats to his mountain life, leaving the stage behind. His life in seclusion is not shown by Mitterer, but the play cannot be said to be open-ended either, since we know what happened to his life model, Leo Reuß. Reality and the theater are not so divided as the director of Mitterer's play would have them.

The Reuß-Kirsch story is framed by two literary references, given expression in *Lions' Den* in recited excerpts from Shakespeare's *Merchant of Venice* and, in the published version of Mitterer's play, G. E. Lessing's dramatic poem, *Nathan the Wise* (see editor's note, pp. 82-83). In both classic plays Jews play the central role, but their attitudes and beliefs are very different. Shylock wants vengeance; Nathan is forgiving. Both men have endured being terrorized, humiliated and persecuted by their fellows. Shylock believes himself justified in exacting revenge on Antonio by cutting a pound of flesh from his debtor's chest, "close to the heart," when he says:

> He hath disgraced me, and
> hindered me half a million; laughed at my losses,
> mocked at my gains, scorned my nation, thwarted my
> bargains, cooled my friends, heated mine
> enemies; and what's his reason? I am a Jew. Hath
> not a Jew eyes? hath not a Jew hands, organs,
> dimensions, senses, affections, passions? fed with
> the same food, hurt with the same weapons, subject
> to the same diseases, healed by the same means,
> warmed and cooled by the same winter and summer as
> a Christian is? If you prick us, do we not bleed?
> If you tickle us, do we not laugh? If you poison
> us, do we not die? and if you wrong us, shall we not
> revenge? (III,i)

To understand Shylock's thirst for revenge in context, one should be aware of prevailing anti-Semitic feelings in Shakespeare's time. Jews were not well liked by the British, and many were suspicious of them. In the figure of Barabas, Christopher Marlow portrayed in his play, *The Jew of Malta* (ca. 1592), a Jewish merchant who had lost all his wealth to the Christians. He is full of unrelenting hate and bent on revenge. He is a villain, wicked, evil and greedy, and he commits brutal acts against the people who are responsible for his ruin, even causing the death of his daughter, Abigail, who had the temerity to be in love with a Christian. At about this time an incident occurred that had the effect of intensifying anti-Semitic sentiments: in 1594 Roderigo Lopez, the physician-in-chief to Queen Elizabeth and a Jew who had converted to Christianity, was convicted of poisoning the Queen. He was hanged the same year.[3] Shakespeare was under the influence of this play while writing *The Merchant of Venice* (ca. 1598).

Nathan too has suffered; Christians have murdered his wife and seven sons in his brother's house. At first he is full of hate, but rather than seek revenge he is able to forgive. He adopts a baby girl given to him wrapped in a coat, seeing in it an act of God who has returned to him one child for the seven he lost. He tells his story to the Friar:

> And when you came,
> Three nights had I in dust and ashes lain
> Before my God and wept – aye, and at times
> Arraigned my maker, raged, and cursed myself
> And the whole world, and to Christianity
> Swore unrelenting hate.
> ....
> But by degrees returning reason came,
> She spake with gentle voice –And yet God is,
> And this was his decree – now exercise
> What thou hast long imagined, and what surely
> Is not more difficult to exercise
> Than to imagine – if thou will it once.
> I rose and called out – God, I will – I will.
> (IV,7; Tr. William Taylor)

It seems Mitterer's protagonist Kirsch must forever decide which side he's on – that of the vengeful Shylock or the forgiving Nathan. In the published version of the German play, he embodies Nathan's conciliatory spirit, while in other versions, such as the translation offered here, he is closer to Shylock. To be sure, both outlooks still exist in our day, always in uneasy counterpoise, and in each production it is up to the play's director to select one of them.

In the Lions' Den contains many elements associated with the Baroque tradition, specifically those exhibited by the Austrian drama, in particular the intermingling of *Schein und Sein*, or appearance and essence. Grillparzer's plays come to mind and, closer to our own time, the plays of Arthur Schnitzler, especially his political play set on the eve of the French Revolution, *The Green Cockatoo*, in which illusion and reality are so seamlessly intermingled that the reader/audience is left wondering what the real truth is. Schnitzler's play also embodies another Baroque tradition: the play within a play, just as we find it in the work commissioned for the Viennese Theater in der Josefstadt, Mitterer's *Panther* (2007).

There is, however, one major difference between Mitterer's two plays: While *In the Lions' Den* takes place in 1936, *The Panther* is situated in our own time and takes up an issue of concern to many of us. The population in Austria (as well as Germany) is getting older and thus more prone to diseases, including dementia and Alzheimer's disease. The estimated life expectancy for men in Austria is 76.6 years, that for women 82.5 years. Because the birth rate is falling, that part of the total population made up of seniors is increasing, even as the number of caregivers decreases. This presents many psychological, economic and political problems.

Felix Mitterer had previously addressed the problematic life of the elderly in his one-act play, *Visiting Hours* (1985), and in the monologue play, *Siberia* (1989),[4] the latter depicting an old man wasting away in a rest home. He is dehumanized, exiled from his home and only occasionally visited by his son.[5] The plight of the elderly is also shown in his play, *The Panther*, the title stemming from Rilke's poem of the same name.

In the drama Marion Liebherr, who must be in her seventies, drives home from the funeral of a man she believes to be her husband. She runs into an old man, injuring his leg. She is not sure if this man has intentionally walked into her car, or if it was her own carelessness. She fears the possible consequences should the man report the accident to the police, since her supposed nephew, a money manager in a bank who is married and in debt, has had her placed under an interdiction order revoking her driver's license. She offers money to the apparently injured man, but he refuses. In their conversation it becomes more and more apparent that these two elderly people share common memories, that they are somehow related. The woman had been married for over fifty years, as had the man, but he tells her that he did not have a happy union. The man tells her he cannot watch a colored TV-screen because of his sensitive eyes, whereupon the woman informs him that her husband had suffered from the same affliction, leaving them to watch TV only in black and white. Curiously, the man also knows where the cognac bottle is, and when he asks for a cigarette, the woman lights one and hands it to him. This oddly homey atmosphere is interrupted by the arrival of a young man who, the woman informs us, is the son of her husband's brother, but, as she confides to the old man later on, is only interested in getting his hands on her money. The old man, who at first is without a name, later introduces himself as Dr. Georg Altmann literally "old man") and exposes the nephew as a con artist. He is subsequently exposed as a trickster himself because he is *not* Dr. Altmann. He explains that he had been living, subsisting really, in an old-age home and wanted to escape. He saw an opportunity to do so when his roommate, a Dr. Altmann, passed away. He took Altmann's medical chart, allowing the latter to be buried under *his* name, which means that the woman at the funeral actually did not bury her husband, who is still very much alive. In his youth this man had been known as "the panther" because he was strong and full of energy. He was also a lady's man, as his real name, Liebherr, unmistakably suggests: a man of or for love. At the end these two finally recognize each other, and it is the "panther poem" by Rilke that plays the central role in this recognition.

 The logical sequence of this play is not easy to follow because *Schein und Sein* are so intermingled that one cannot be sure of the true identity of the characters. They claim to be people they are not. The confusion approaches vertigo since the man does not even know who he is, or, if he does, one cannot be sure he's not playing the assumed identity in order to punish his wife, who had put him in the old age home. Marion feels that this is the case when she accuses him of playing a play within a play, a tactic she interprets as a kind of "revenge"– a charge he vehemently denies because for a play one needs planning, of which he is no longer capable. Mitterer supports this point in his stage directions, which indicate that the man really does not know what is going on. Marion indicates that she too is playing a game, for the purpose of doing penance.

In all this confusion, the general impression is created that these two are more than mere acquaintances, that they have actually known each other for a long time. The reader and the audience sense that this is the case, but as of yet there is no certainty. Did this man cause the accident himself by running into Marion's car because he wanted to return home? One may assume this to be the case. When Marion remarks that he showed great agility in rolling himself off the car, he replies that he had been very good at such maneuvers in his youth, having been gifted with remarkable athletic ability. And does he speak the truth when he asserts that he is a terrible man, an egotistical bastard? One could agree here with the remark of their nephew that he has no idea what is going on. One possible point of view is that the events are described not directly but indirectly, from the inner world of the characters, and it is quite apparent that this world is highly confused. The man has dementia, which makes it difficult for him to distinguish events. But Marion too seems slightly demented, and her "nephew" suggests a few times that she leave her place and go to an old age home. All this makes it difficult for her to differentiate between reality and illusion, although clearly the man's dementia has progressed further than hers.

Marion wants to "shock" the man back to reality, thereby helping him to remember. This is one of the highlights of the play because the tactic she uses is one that is helpful not only in the specific case presented here on the illusory stage but in the real world as well. Marion confronts the man with psychological photographs, so to speak; she tells him, in the third person, of many experiences she shared with her husband, hoping he might connect. She reminisces about their life together, conjuring up their common past, describing, for instance, how he gradually became more and more confused, began to forget where he put things, accused her of taking things away from him, lost the ability to find his way home and kept running into moving cars. Finally, he forgot her name entirely and addressed her by the name of his mistress. The situation only worsened after their son's tragic accident. He would not come home for days, staying rather with a woman younger than Marion.

The man seems to agree with everything Marion tells him. He is aware at times that his memory is faulty, as he admits to her. He can only recall fragments of events. His power of reflection is severely damaged. Mitterer indicates as much in a separate scene in which the man looks at his own reflection in the mirror, prompting him to cry out that he can no longer stand it, whereupon he smashes the mirror with his stick. The mirror reflects not only his outer image but also his inner condition. Mitterer had come across a similar mirror image in a poem by Victor Fritz which he included in an anthology. In translation this poem reads:

Empty mirror
You look into the mirror,
The mirror is empty.
You have no face. You see 'It' no more.
Your person is gone
Into nothingness.

> You cannot find yourself
> In the empty mirror.
> You are afraid in front of the emptiness.
> Your void.
> The void, it is everything and nothing. (Tr. G.K.S.)[6]

The decline of the mental powers in both characters is also indicated by Mitterer's deft use of light effects. When Marion returns home from the funeral she remarks that there was much darkness on the way, and the man agrees with this double-entendre remark, referring as it does to the time of day as well as to their mental states. The light falling into the room in the first scene is a "dim winter light." The room is lighted by candles, and at the end of the play there is total darkness. These light effects help to underscore the failing mental acuity of these two people, who yearn to lift the veil of darkness from their memories.

Marion is more and more convinced that the man across from her is her husband, and she continues to try to shock him into reality. She reminds him of their lost son, not naming him at first, just alluding to some young man who had committed suicide. She forces him to put a name to this youth of nineteen and also offer a reason why he killed himself. The man cannot remember, but she presses on. The man replies that one who loses a son feels guilty for the rest of his life. Then he nearly breaks down, and the wife retreats by insisting that he did not cause the death of the young man. But he confesses to feeling guilty nonetheless. The woman tries to break down the barriers he raises, a strategy reflected, for instance, in the tactic of addressing him with the familiar *du,* which he promptly rejects, pushing her back to the formal *Sie.*[7]

The woman does not give up, however. She knows that "The Panther" by Rilke was her husband's favorite poem, one he knew by heart, having recited it many times over the years. The change comes not by forcing the issue but by calling up the power of love. They talk about Paris, the proverbial city of love, where they had spent happy days together. They listen to the song of Maurice Chevalier, "Paris, je t'aime d'amour." Slowly the man's memory returns, and he asks her if he has ever been in that city. And now they recite the Rilke poem together, and whenever the man's memory fails him, his wife supplies the next line:

> From time to time the curtain of the eye
> is quietly raised – an image then appears,
> goes through the limbs in silence, tension high,
> and, once within the heart, it clears.
> (Tr. Mike Lyons and Patrick Drysdale)

This scene shows that the two clearly belong together, and in the last scene the man knows with certainty that the woman next to him is his wife. His recognition is accentuated by his use of the familiar address form, heretofore rejected: "Du … bist meine Frau…?" [You are my wife?]. Thomas Liebherr was not quite sure, but now he recognizes her as his wife. This is his transformation from the doubting Thomas to one who knows and believes. Alas, the interlude of clarity lasts but a moment, and in the final scene he puts money and the checkbook on the table and disappears, leaving his wife to run after him.

The catalyst for restoring the man's memory, though it be for a short time, is the Rilke poem. Mitterer dramatizes the poem, and the similarities between man and animal are striking. The panther is caged up in the zoo, just as Thomas Liebherr is confined to the old age home. The panther is isolated, and is no longer is stimulated, much like the man. Both are bored and lonely. The panther paces back and forth in its confinement, that being all it can do, all it is allowed to do. Both waste away in their captivity. Only now and then does an image penetrate the eye of the panther and go straight to its heart. This is also a way of describing the man's fragmented experience. But the man can escape from his prison while the panther cannot.

The ending is left to the reader's or the audience's imagination. It may be assumed, however, that the man, after having experienced the bliss of recognition and having felt the love of his wife, decides to end his life voluntarily. He tells Marion that she should not return him to the institution from which he has escaped. He very likely will run into a car again, and next time he will not recover. Mitterer uses car accidents a few times in this play: the man himself has had several traffic accidents, and the nephew has had one as well. We also know that dementia or Alzheimer's disease is progressive, and, with the memory of this man almost totally gone, he can no longer be the subject of any play. What remains is the substrate of love and a successful homecoming. Although the stage is enveloped in total darkness at the end, the red rose glowing on the table is the last thing to fade.

What Felix Mitterer shows us in this work is not only the fate of a single person, or two people, but of the many who will certainly find themselves in the same situation, afflicted with the mental disease of age. With the rising quality of modern medicine and nutrition, the number of these people is also rising. With this play Mitterer asks us how literature can contribute to a better understanding of such disease and perhaps even demonstrate ways of helping its victims. The same question was posed by the writer, Siegfried Lenz; his suggestion was that writers write with openness and love towards these people, and, when this was not possible, compassion.[8]

Mitterer incorporates literary classics into both plays. In so doing, he shows us that these old works are not outdated but highly relevant for our own time. After having read or seen a Mitterer play, one might be moved to reread Shakespeare's *Merchant of Venice,* Lessing's dramatic poem, *Nathan the Wise,* Schiller's patriotic drama, *Wilhelm Tell,* or Rilke's poem, "The Panther," and find oneself with a new appreciation of these masterpieces. They continue to speak to us in our own time; and they engage the reader regardless of the time that has passed between their original creation and our era.

Gerd K. Schneider
Syracuse University

Notes

[1] Mitterer is very careful in choosing names for his characters. The case can be made that he modeled the name of Kirsch on that of Helmut Hirsch, a German Jew, who was executed in Berlin at about the time in which Mitterer's play is set. Hirsch was accused of a bombing plot for the purpose of destabilizing the German Reich.

[2] The real Reuß did not play the protagonist's role in Schiller's drama while he was in Germany or Austria; he did portray the character in 1939 in Los Angeles – in English.

[3] See James Shapiro, *Shakespeare and the Jews* (New York: Columbia Press, 1996).

[4] The English translation was published in 1994 by Ariadne Press in the collection *Siberia and Other Plays.*

[5] For an analysis see Gerd K. Schneider, "Timely Meditations or Not Yet! Social Criticism in Felix Mitterer's *Siberia," Felix Mitterer:*

A Critical Introduction, ed. Nicholas J. Meyerhofer and Karl E. Webb (Riverside: Ariadne Press, 1995) 195-205.

[6] Viktor Fritz, "Reflexion," *Texte aus der Innenwelt,* ed. Felix Mitterer (Vienna: Czernin Verlag, 2001).

[7] This grammatical distinction is, in my opinion, nearly impossible to render into English because the personal pronoun in both cases is "you." Another Austrian dramatist, Arthur Schnitzler, uses the same technique in his play, *Reigen,* or *La Ronde,* in scene nine, in which the actress tries to seduce the count.

[8] Siegfried Lenz, "Die Darstellung des Alters in der Literatur," *Über den Schmerz* (Hamburg: Hoffmann und Campe, 1998) 94-95.